Repression
and Resistance

Latin American Perspectives Series

Ronald H. Chilcote, Series Editor

† Available in hardcover and paperback.

Repression and Resistance

The Struggle for Democracy in Central America

Edelberto Torres-Rivas

Westview Press
Boulder, San Francisco, & London

Latin American Perspectives Series, Number 6

Originally published as *Centroamérica: La Democracia Posible,* © 1987 FLACSO-EDUCA

Copyright © 1989 by Westview Press, Inc.

Published in 1989 in the United States of America by Westview Press, Inc., 5500 Central Avenue, Boulder, Colorado 80301, and in the United Kingdom by Westview Press, Inc., 13 Brunswick Centre, London WC1N 1AF, England

Library of Congress Cataloging-in-Publication Data
Torres-Rivas, Edelberto.
  Repression and resistance : the struggle for democracy in Central
America / Edelberto Torres-Rivas.
    p. cm.—(Latin American perspectives series; no. 6)
  Translation of *Centroamérica: La Democracia Posible.*
  Includes bibliographies and index.
  ISBN 0-8133-7654-8
  1. Central America—Politics and government—1979–   . 2. Social
conflict—Central America—History. 3. Oligarchy—Central America—
History. 4. Government, Resistance to—Central America—History.
5. Representative government and representation—Central America—
History. I. Title. II. Series.
F1439.5.T67 1989
320.9728—dc19   89-5313
                                                                                  CIP

Printed and bound in the United States of America

(∞) The paper used in this publication meets the requirements of the American National
      Standard for Permanence of Paper for Printed Library Materials Z39.48-1984.

10   9   8   7   6   5   4   3   2   1

Contents

Acknowledgments

Though the original writing of these chapters constituted a great deal of reflection and hard work, their collection in this volume was a far less arduous task for the author. The brunt of that task fell on the translator. As is well known, in the specialized language used by Latin American sociologists, concepts like "populism," "campesino" (peasant farmer), "oligarchy," and "the state" have distinct cultural meanings at times impossible to capture in a single word. Understanding my baroque style of written Spanish and translating it into the more direct mode of English expression has been the valuable accomplishment of my dear colleague and friend, Jeff Sluyter. My deepest thanks to him and once again to my wife, Cecilia—whose advice and tenderness help me so much.

Edelberto Torres-Rivas
San José

1
Introduction

Seeds of the Regional Crisis

The origins and evolution of the Central American crisis have in recent years demanded our attention more powerfully than ever, as much for that crisis's originality as for the vitality of the forces actively involved. Analyses produced to date have displayed both quantitative abundance and a wide variety of approaches. What has been created, then, is something unknown before the contemporary period: a body of literature about the crisis.

The magnitude of the political turmoil—especially since the Sandinista rupture of July 1979—has imbued the analysis with an exceptionally urgent quality. And that urgency to understand the entire course of events has created an almost irresistible tension, leading to the production of *textos de circunstancias*, or "instant books," as they have been called in English. Those books, in turn, have been destined for a reading public whose interest is directly proportional to its lack of knowledge. The risk in responding to that urgency is that the author's ideological separation from the present may be poorly achieved, that the separation from immediate surroundings required by all knowledge—in order to filter out the secondary, the circumstantial, and the emotional—may not be established.

Throughout the five essays brought together in this book I was aware of those risks. Thus I attempted to trace contemporary developments to their deepest historical roots while interpreting the behavior of the actors for what it was rather than what some might have wished it to be. Social forces were at times embodied by a political movement, confronted by social conflict, or otherwise brought together in order to pursue alternative programs. Sometimes these forces were involved in each of those forms of organization at the same time, and other times they even went beyond them.

Another difficulty exists. The diversity of situations in the five nations produced over a long period of time but reinforced by the effects of the crisis makes it increasingly difficult to consider Central America as a regional unity. That is, establishing a *general* analytic hypothesis, compatible with the heterogeneity of nationally specific situations, would hardly be an easy task. To speak of a "regional crisis" can lead to abuses of excess in some cases, and of insufficiency in others.

If we consider the nature of the economic crisis, for example, we find that it is international, impacting on all of the countries in the region. Nevertheless, due to specific circumstances of the political crisis, the effects have been more negative in Nicaragua and El Salvador than in Guatemala or Costa Rica.

Similarly, from a political-military viewpoint, the presence in El Salvador and Nicaragua of armed opposition forces—which have been difficult to defeat in both countries, though for opposite reasons—confers on those societies dimensions approaching economic chaos and social dissolution. In contrast, Honduras and Costa Rica have not experienced— in terms of either duration or depth—the kind of political violence and civil war that has affected the other three countries of the region.

But what Central American countries probably do have in common is a history as underdeveloped societies within a particular geographic region of the U.S. sphere of influence. And that is exactly what constitutes the "explanatory axis" of any responsible analysis of a Central American crisis that has affected the region's political, social, and ideological structure. As we will see, it was the persistence of oligarchic components within that structure that gave rise to the crisis of the contemporary period.

Latin American literature has frequently dealt with "the crisis of oligarchic domination." That phrase has been used, from multiple perspectives, to refer to the phenomena that had gradually been altering the monopolistic control of power enjoyed for decades by commercial- agricultural groups.

Originally, the state, the economy, and the society itself were placed at the service of local interests, which established links with the global capitalist market through the export of primary products. However, the dynamic axis gradually began to change, strengthening itself more and more within the domestic market. In South America that process generally took place in the 1930s, though with slight variations from country to country.

But in Central America, that process did not begin until the post– World War II period. For good or ill, it soon became evident that the oligarchic, authoritarian, and exclusivist style of domination had begun to fall apart. Changes were most obvious among the sponsors of social integration, among the various kinds of political movements that had begun to appear, and with the unprecedented nature of internal conflicts— the latter phenomena expressing an increasing differentiation within those dominant groups generically referred to as "the oligarchy."

The crisis of the coffee republic—as the oligarchic period is sometimes called—only began to appear clearly in Central America after the end of World War II. And much as happened elsewhere in other regions, the crisis first emerged as a political crisis. That is, the immediately visible expressions of that crisis arose in the spheres of political relations and ideological conflict.

The fall of military dictatorships in Guatemala, El Salvador, and Honduras, as well as that of an increasingly authoritarian regime in Costa Rica—all of which occurred between 1944 and 1948—marked the beginning of that crisis. New social-democratic movements, political parties, and intellectual debate surged to the fore while Central American society, in imbalanced fashion, took on the challenge of modernization.

And it was from that point on that regional heterogeneity became increasingly manifest. The varying responses—in terms of installing less authoritarian or even clearly democratic regimes—were uneven. After 1948 the Costa Rican electoral system was further consolidated under liberal democratic principles. In the ten years that followed World War II Guatemala undertook an initial, notable experiment in social and cultural renovation. In Nicaragua, the Somozas' dictatorship-for-life prevented—through both force and co-optation—the entrance of new social forces onto the political scene.

Democratic change was also blocked by various means in Honduras and El Salvador. But the entire region's economy benefited from the new dynamism of international markets, and what resulted was a reinforcement of the structural foundations—that some observers would qualify as economic—of the oligarchic groups. That dynamism, in turn, was therefore detrimental to the democratic struggles against the oligarchic system of domination.

Underlying Costs of Dependent Development

The preceding discussion, though brief, is important as an aid to understanding the following chapters' analyses and the various interpretations that I will propose in each one. In any case, though it is difficult to summarize the multiple origins of the crisis that Central Americans are suffering today, the whole should be seen within the parameters of a necessary—but incomplete—process of modernization.

The reasons for that relative failure must be sought in both domestic and international factors.

In very general terms, since the decade of the 1950s, criticism of the antioligarchic system has at the same time been a struggle to implant structures of social participation. Indeed, the so-called democratic struggles have always voiced demands for a law-abiding state, for effective universal suffrage, for independent political organization, for a free press, and for freedom of conscience. That is, the leaders of these struggles have pursued liberal manifestations of democracy.

We now know that none of those goals was tolerated by oligarchic power brokers. Their authoritarian character was extremely slow to change, allowing for the emergence of only a very limited form of democracy.

And as I intend to explain in the following pages of this book, the political crisis in Central America—which exploded in the mid-1970s—was born of the defeats suffered by the democratic and reformist political forces of the immediate postwar period. Guerrilla warfare sprang from the failure of reformism. Popular violence (violence perpetrated by the common people) was the response to state violence; one fed the other in a tragic cycle without apparent end.

Projects of political change could have been initiated parallel to economic changes; the so-called development style could have satisfactorily confronted the enormous inequalities inherited from the past. For that reason, in order to understand contemporary Central American history, it is necessary to make at least brief reference to the economic antecedents of the crisis. That is, there must be an analysis of the manner in which the economic system—with its agro-export base—became modified, in what directions, and in response to the impulse of which social forces.

Beginning in about 1950 the regional economy experienced a period of significant growth, which lasted for more than twenty-five years. The gross domestic product (GDP) grew at an average annual rate of 5.3 percent—higher than the average of Latin America as a whole. That rate was also significantly higher than the rate of population growth. By 1970 the per capita GDP had increased more than 80 percent in relation to 1950. These statistics both indicate the relative importance of the change and reveal its comparative limits. During the same period in the United States, for example, per capita income increased 400 percent.

The industrial sector's contribution to GDP rose from 13.3 percent in 1960 to 18.1 percent in 1970, due to the stimuli created by the Central American Common Market (CACM), which in reality was nothing more than a successful regional free trade zone. The new industry consisted above all of the production of immediate consumption goods, but it also initiated the formation of a manufacturing base through import substitution mechanisms.

Those years—especially since the end of the 1950s—were also very favorable to the modernization of export agriculture. Significant additions to the brief list of traditional export products (primarily coffee and bananas) included cotton, sugar, and beef, almost all of which were headed for the North American market.

The introduction of those new agricultural preferences changed the agrarian structure, making it ever more mechanized and capital oriented. But the ensuing expansion also increased the considerable inequalities already existing between the export sector and campesino forms of agriculture, where family-based subsistence farming and basic grain production—for popular, domestic consumption—were combined in order to survive.

The underlying nature of that economic growth is what must be well understood, because statistical indicators by themselves explain very little. The expansion of manufacturing meant that the commercial deficit increased, since that expansion implied the import of high-priced manufactured products—in exchange for raw materials as well as semifinished and capital goods—in proportions greater than those that could have been compensated by the region's rising exports.

In commercial terms, whereas the region's 1960 trade balance registered a deficit of less than $83 million, by 1970 that deficit had risen to $226 million. That is, the deficit increased together with industrial expansion, as a result of the openness of the region's economies to international trade. Again, it must be noted that the agricultural sector was the one— in the best as well as the worst of years—that financed current and capital account imbalances, via its consistent trade surpluses.

However, the social problems that have been produced by that dependent model are even more dramatic. The modernization of export agriculture was accomplished literally at the cost of campesino lands, which were expropriated either violently or "discreetly," depending on the moment and the location of capital expansion.

With the expansion of cotton cultivation, for example, campesinos were expropriated along the Pacific coast of Guatemala, El Salvador, and Nicaragua. Meanwhile, cattle raising (beef production) took campesino lands in various other geographic zones—especially in Guatemala, Honduras, and Nicaragua—in a process that affected more than two million people. As is well known, the essence of the social problems of Central America since the mid-1970s has been the question of *land*— its distribution and cultivation. Campesino struggles to defend their land, and later those to recover that land, have marked the history of the region.

In order to illustrate the way in which the land question underlies the regional crisis, we will consider—as one of many possible examples—the problems experienced in the labor market. When Guatemala and El Salvador initiated the industrialization process within the framework of the CACM's program of economic integration, in 1960, urban unemployment in both countries was about 12 percent. However, population growth far surpassed the levels of employment creation, especially in the countryside. For Central America as a whole, the economically active population increased at an average annual rate of 2.4 percent, while the population grew at a rate of 3.1 percent. Industrial expansion—at an annual rate of 8.4 percent—was incapable of providing jobs for a rapidly swelling urban population of working-age adults. That population's rapid growth was due primarily to the vast number of people who, expelled from the countryside, had no other choice but to migrate to the cities.

In effect, industry itself was not responsible for unemployment. Rather, it was largely a consequence of the simultaneous combination of two circumstances. On the one hand, there was the incapacity of the agricultural sector to absorb a significant part of the work force—despite considerable export-crop expansion—or to retain that population via various means of reorganizing patterns of land tenure. The latter type of solution was proposed by neither governments nor the agrarian bourgeoisie. On the other hand, industrial growth was capital- rather than labor-intensive—based therefore on that which was most expensive and scarce in the region, rather than responding to employment needs.

The quantitative importance of economic growth did not reflect the social effects of that process. Though the social stratification of society was gradually modified, the amount of poverty increased significantly throughout the isthmus. The economy's growth was achieved to the benefit of a minority, as almost every study of Central America produced in recent years has repeatedly demonstrated. Sometimes that reality has been concealed behind statistical indicators such as "per capita national income."

But social development is of a qualitative nature and therefore needs to be interpreted and judged with other analytical tools. How does one explain, for example, that while GDP grew, poverty actually increased? The wealthiest 5 percent of the population saw their incomes rise at a rate fifteen times greater than that of the poorest 50 percent of the population. In 1977 the Economic Commission for Latin America (ECLA) estimated that 65 percent of the Central American people were living in an extremely perilous situation in which it was impossible for them to acquire in sufficient amounts life's necessities: food, housing, clothing, and education.

Moving Beyond Descriptive Analysis

Based on the preceding comments, it might appear that the political crisis in Central America—particularly in Nicaragua, El Salvador, and Guatemala—originated in an accumulation of misery, and that the reaction to that situation had been "the revolution of the poor." But we know that it did not happen that way. Clearly, poverty led to discontent, but desperation does not always acquire the conscious forms of organized political protest that appeared in the region. In other words, the analysis must go beyond objective description and explore subjective factors.

The essays brought together in this book attempt to offer explanations of many issues raised by the crisis. Chapter 2 contains a series of assertions, often presented in the form of hypotheses, which are intended to serve as the foundations of an interpretation of Central American history from 1930 to the present. In that chapter, a distinction is made between the political and the economic aspects of the crisis in order to examine the various ways in which the two have affected the traditional oligarchic system of domination—a system of undisputed monopolistic control, over a period of many years, by the lords of the land.

The general proposition is that the historical rupture represented by "Sandinismo" is in effect the conjunction of two crises—the old one (of the traditional oligarchic system) and a new one (affecting the capitalist system and its political offspring). That second chapter was published in *Centroamérica: Más Allá de la Crisis*, edited by D. Castillo Rivas (Ediciones SIAP, México, 1983).

Chapter 3 focuses on an analysis of the revolutionary popular movements as a form of social movement capable of joining together a diversity of class-based groups. Those movements are also marked by a confluence of diverse ideological orientations, unified by a shared condition as "politically subordinated sectors" and convinced—within the limits created by the failures of democratic aspirations—that armed struggle is the only possible response. The *disorder* that accompanies the political crisis, in effect, is seen as a creation of the forces of *order*. This third chapter was originally published in *La Crisis Centroamericana*, a book edited by Daniel Camacho and Manuel Rojas (FLACSO-EDUCA, San José, 1984).

In that third chapter, Central America is viewed in allegorical fashion as the recipient of all the evils that escaped from Pandora's box. Though its analysis refers either directly or indirectly to El Salvador, Guatemala, and Nicaragua rather than to the entire region, the themes discussed are very closely related to those examined in the fourth chapter, "Eight

Keys to Understanding the Central American Crisis." In the latter chapter, however, the international dimension is included for the first time.

Though the chapter's major focus is on the internal dynamics of the crisis, the international aspects are obviously of great importance. And at that level the Nicaraguan crisis revealed, among other things, that the fall of Somoza was the failure of U.S. foreign policy in the region. Moreover, that failure exposed a changing international reality: the direct and sudden entrance of international forces into the Central American political equation, which occurred together with the relative weakening of United States hegemony.

As is exceedingly natural, relations between that superpower and the Central American region have been asymmetrical. In early 1930, speaking undoubtedly with great precision, a senior State Department official said that no Central American president would be stable without U.S. diplomatic recognition. And over the more than fifty years since then, the North American capacity to tolerate processes of change—processes that are of course beyond U.S. control—has been put to the test. Among those troublesome processes has been everything from simple political reform to economic modernization.

The destabilization of the Jacobo Arbenz government in Guatemala in 1954 was evidence of those difficulties in developing positive relations with reformist forces. In El Salvador, the pressures against the civil-military junta that lasted from December 1960 to January 1961 favored Lieutenant Colonel Julio Rivera's coup d'état. The crimes in that Salvadoran case had been a rural literacy program and a more liberal electoral law.

Though there were favorable pressures during the Alliance for Progress period, the reforms that were finally accepted helped to construct a security apparatus in the hands of the army and never contributed to any real agrarian reform. The reformist program of the first General Oswaldo López Arellano government in Honduras failed because of a combination of U.S. pressures and the complaints of large landowners. One could continue in similar chronological fashion all the way to the Reagan administration, with its policies of open and direct intervention in Central American politics. Chapter 4 has appeared in "Ocho claves para comprender la crisis política de Centroamérica," in *Polémica*, No. 1, San José, Costa Rica, 1981.

In Chapter 5 my intent is to delve into the history of Nicaragua in order to explain why the Sandinistas were able to triumph as a revolutionary option despite the existence of a "third force" acting in the latter period of the resolution of the crisis (the first half of 1979). To study the roots of that crisis is to examine the history of the Somoza family as a power elite. The title of the chapter, "The State Against Society: The Roots of the Nicaraguan Revolution," is a reference to the degree of isolation with which the second Somoza protected himself. It might have been better to call it "The Frightened Sultan: Everyone, Including Part of His Court, Is Against Him." That fifth chapter was published in *La Crisis del Poder en Centroamérica* (EDUCA, San José, 1983), an earlier collection of the author's essays.

The final chapter is the one most directly related to the book's title and consists of reflections that revolve around two central ideas—ideas that have been debated but too often forgotten. The first of those ideas is that no democratic model exists that is suitable for imitation; no democratic experience is irrelevant to others, but neither can those experiences be copied.

The second idea is that democracy is a social product requiring a preceding process of historical construction. As a consequence, beyond the "formalities of democracy" (constitutions, elections), substantive social and economic content must be created—to the degree made possible by the entirety of forces dedicated to its contruction. In other words, though democracy is a historic form of organizing consensus, it is not aimed exclusively at choosing via the ballot box those who should govern.

Here it is important to recognize that the authoritarian system is a particularly violent form of ordered society, a system that has overseen the evolution of Central American societies while occasionally exhibiting many of the superficial attributes of liberal democracy.

This last chapter is of a preliminary nature and contains proposals for discussion at a time and place where political polemics are less intense. It was published in the book of the same title, *Centroamérica: La Democracia Posible* (FLACSO-EDUCA, San José, 1987).

The publication of these essays in English represents an effort to have a Central American interpretation of the crisis reach the English-speaking public. It is, in effect, a collection of reflections about the region's critical situation by one of its kindred sons.

2

The Two Crises in Central America: Some Hypotheses

All political crises, viewed in summary fashion, consist of a common set of characteristics. As Nicos Poulantzas has recognized,[1] these shared characteristics mark the class struggle of any society in which a certain general equilibrium between contending social groups has broken down. In order for this to happen, however, the social dimensions of the breakdown must be so extensive that they impact directly on all sectors of society that have been organized on a national scale. In other words, not only must social relations—understood as inclusive of their political, economic, and ideological aspects—be affected; rather, beyond that point, the guaranteed privileges serving to maintain the system's normal reproduction have to be altered.

Therefore, explanations that reduce the concept of political crisis to the secretive world of power—to a type of class-based political power expressed by the state as ultimate authority—prove to be insufficient. The analysis must be able to determine factors that explain the disruption of commitments contracted between class interests in the political sphere. More specifically, the analysis must reveal the reasons why frictions arise within alliances between those groups or class factions that compose what has been called the society's "structure of domination." In any case, the analysis should not merely, nor even necessarily, deal with the power of the state.

Furthermore, the crisis can only be seen as revolutionary when the rupture in political relations affects all elements that form the class base of the state's power. The analysis cannot, therefore, be limited to the state (defined as the combined bureaucratic-repressive apparatus and the system of norms that sanction those functions[2]). For the state is nothing more than the institutional expression of those political relations.

In Central America, in effect, the fragile nature of the loyalties created in order to maintain some people subservient to others was combined with elite unwillingness to share power with the subordinate classes. These two factors must also be recognized as fundamental elements affecting social institutions both in their formative stages and in the current period of crisis. Those institutions include political parties, the church, the mass media, the unions, the schools, and the family.

In the most fundamental sense, the Central American political crisis centers upon those social relations that have been generated by the dependent capitalist system of production, for that system underlies class domination. The common vision of Marxism would explain the misfortunes of the political superstructure as a more or less sophisticated reflection of what is occurring at the economic base. This chapter, however, will attempt to examine the present critical processes from a perspective that focuses on the entire system of domination in Central America, and to explain how all of this has led, as a consequence, to revolutionary crisis.

This type of crisis is at once a challenge to state power and a consequence of the weakness of that power, because the state is the institutional crux of the system of class domination.[3] It must be understood, therefore, that the processes taking place are more than a mere "reflection" of the movements within the economic structure. This does not mean, however, that those movements do not form part of the explanation that I am attempting to give. Indeed the economic structure should be viewed as the origin of as much as the consequence of political actions.

This proposition will perhaps only gain acceptance through a reconstruction of the notion that society is a contradictory totality in a continual state of flux. Within that notion, the economic dimension is a decisive element of any analysis and/or explanatory presentation. With this theoretical foundation in mind, therefore, it is worthwhile to examine the nature of Central American society—as well as the consequences of the crisis that have affected that society since 1930—in a more concrete, historical manner.

The Reinforcement of Oligarchic Domination

It is widely accepted today that the crisis of 1929–1930, in terms of its impact on Central American society, was of an essentially economic nature. Internally this impact took the form of a decline in production, the effects of which continued long after 1930. The immediate costs of that recession were unquestionably less severe than its effective duration. Indeed, the crisis was not felt locally in a financial sense as a catastrophe drastically interrupting the internal lines of production. Rather, its primary consequence was a long-term period of stagnation, which only began to ease toward the end of World War II.

What was a genuine financial earthquake in other parts of the world, therefore, meant little more than a gradual regression in the case of Central America. Undoubtedly, this difference was due to the agricultural character of society and to the nature of externally directed economic ties established via international trade. That is, a relatively measured decline occurred because of the specific nature of the region's agrarian structure. That structure, in turn, was predominantly based upon small private plots and large landed estates.

The small-farming sector's capacity to absorb the unemployed rural masses was tested in the years following the crisis of 1929–1930. Refuge offered by the campesino economy signified, in effect, a process of social involution. Therefore, as has often occurred in typical monoexporting economies, the Great Depression led to a partial reduction of monetary activity in the region's domestic markets. This decline was due to a sharp drop in external demand, which in better times provided the driving force of the local economies. In any case, the consequences of that decline were not catastrophic.

At this point it makes sense to recall the cyclical price fluctuations to which primary-export products (in this case, coffee) are subjected in international markets. Periods of boom are inevitably followed by periods of pressure on preceding price levels. In dependent economies, these fluctuations themselves can neither raise nor reduce the salaries of the work force. Nor can they affect general conditions in the workplace, for these conditions are determined by internal factors established by oligarchical social and cultural structures.

The living standards of the campesino population were therefore confined to the limits of a subsistence economy, in which the consumption of basic goods is a function of local supply. Unemployment, though less visible in the countryside—where 80 percent of the population lived during the 1930s—existed nonetheless in all sectors of the national economy.

Meanwhile agricultural "businessmen"—landowners with varying levels of capital holdings—were able to continue operating despite a drop in income. Accumulation was achieved, in this case, through either the expansion of landholdings or the amassing of material wealth itself (rather than capital). In this way the landowning structure was able to absorb part, though not all, of the owners' income losses without

Table 1
Central America: Coffee Production and Export Levels (1929-1945, in millions of pounds)

Year	Production	Exports	Year	Production	Exports
1929/30	329	276	1937/38	356	351
1930/31	344	343	1938/39	354	316
1931/32	286	288	1939/40	341	306
1932/33	346	250	1940/41	319	294
1933/34	286	298	1941/42	378	261
1934/35	323	295	1942/43	375	305
1935/36	326	297	1943/44	344	317
1936/37	402	300	1944/45	370	316

Source: *The World's Coffee*, No. 9, FAO, Rome, Italy, 1947, pp. 98-116.

significantly affecting those resources destined for the expansion of production.

However, the extraordinary profits generated by the rental of land continued independent of falling profit levels in the export sector. Coffee production was maintained to a great extent by the weak status of the *colono* (agricultural worker), in Guatemala, El Salvador, and Nicaragua, and that of the small private producer, particularly in Costa Rica. In both instances, coffee growers avoided the annoyance of having to pay salaries and were left with merely the marginal production costs required for the maintenance and reproduction of the work force.

What occurred was not so much a spectacular collapse of regional production or exports as it was a zigzagging stagnation of more than fifteen years duration (see Table 1). The figures remind one of a snake whose head and tail move without altering the level of its body.

In the five years following the crash of 1929 the price of coffee fell, on average, by an amount equivalent to 50 percent of its previous monetary value. Though this caused coffee growers to suffer serious losses of income, their personal state of health was hardly jeopardized. Nevertheless, the slackness of international demand inevitably affected the entire social structure, including its uppermost strata.[4]

This chapter's *first proposition* is that the crisis of the system of oligarchic domination and of its corresponding institutional manifestation, the liberal state, did not begin during the 1930s as in some Latin American societies. To the contrary, the global capitalist crisis—which spread to other countries via international trade, commercial credits, and financial intermediation—left the social bases of the oligarchy's political predominance intact. In effect, the crisis only reinforced those social bases.

Though protests of various sorts took place, they did not achieve a definitive erosion of the political order. The campesino insurrection of 1932 in El Salvador is perhaps the best example. Other important challenges to the system included Augusto César Sandino's nationalist movement, from 1927 to 1932 in Nicaragua, and the "great strike" of the United Fruit Company's banana workers in Costa Rica, in 1934.

The entire region experienced a period of stagnation that lasted more than fifteen years[5] before gradually ending between 1945 and 1948. That period naturally had regressive effects on the economy. But the system of domination was able to resist those effects of the crisis by applying traditional measures of control, including political exclusion and violent repression of the popular masses, and in particular, of the campesinos.

These measures implied permanent forms of institutionalized violence in conjunction with restrictions on civil rights, such as the elimination of political parties and the limitation or prohibition of trade union organizing. Executive power was predominant, personalized, and arbitrary. The authoritarian vise, persistent since the colonial era, tightened once again on the social and political life of the region.

By assuming the role of the oligarchy's armed right hand, caudillos (military leaders) placed themselves at the summit of political power in each country, with the exception of Costa Rica. Their justifying credo repeated the old, familiar formula of sacrificing social progress to "order," whose value reigns supreme in backward agrarian societies.

The regimes that presided over Guatemala, El Salvador, Honduras, and Nicaragua—after the successive illegitimate reelections of Generals Jorge Ubico, Maximiliano Hernández Martínez, Tiburcio Carías Andino, and Anastasio Somoza García—were unadulterated military dictatorships. However, in themselves, they did not constitute a novelty within the annals of Central American history. Those dictatorships were not the cause, then, of the political crisis. In fact they formed part of a continuity, a solution impeding rupture.

My *second proposition* is that the prolonged effects of the economic crisis—including the oligarchy's unwillingness either to allow or to encourage social change—stemmed from political causes. This was due to the conservative, orthodox behavior of the dominant agricultural groups.[6]

The total predominance of the interests of the large landowners—particularly those of the coffee growers—established the boundaries within which economic policy could take shape. The need to defend the political order in turn inspired acceptance of a conservative diagnosis and treatment of the ailing body of the economy. In sum, the governments of the time were responding—through both omission and commission—to deeply rooted oligarchic instincts.

As a result, the eventual moment of economic recovery was delayed, the vitality of the economic recovery was reduced, and its consolidation made more difficult. Deflationary policies, for example, exacerbated the long-term negative effects of the decline in foreign commerce. Worse still were the corresponding restrictions on bank credit, the suspension of public works, and a shrinking national budget.[7] The upshot was an economy paralyzed by a lack of demand in almost every sector. An orthodox, neoclassical economic model induced the oligarchy to neglect supply, to sharply cut public spending, to reduce wages, and to block the possibility of mobilizing financial resources through institutional channels.

The reactivation of the Central American economies occurred only once better conditions for the production and sale of coffee had been reestablished. Rising demand for other export products—particularly bananas—also contributed to that recovery. During the immediate postwar period, from 1945 to 1948, the agrarian-export sector matched its former historic levels, as external factors resumed their previous importance. During this period, the demand for coffee increased and prices rose to new heights. It was also the beginning of the "cotton boom," and North American investments returned as the global capitalist economy enjoyed a brief period of rapid growth. International prices of Central American primary goods—which bore no relation to domestic costs of production—generated an unexpected accumulation of capital, which in turn favored the beginning of a new cycle of expansion.

A *third proposition* springs from the realization that, in the moment marked by the end of the economic crisis, well-known characteristics of oligarchic behavior[8] in the productive sector were reestablished. For reasons that are at the same time directly associated with the period of stagnation, the third proposition suggests that the political crisis began at the very moment of transition between stagnation and recovery. In retrospect, it becomes evident that the economic crisis effectively postponed the political crisis, producing two diverse forms of transition born at different junctures. During this period of sharp increases in exports and of a general loosening of the static sociocultural structure of Central American society, the first real challenges to the traditional oligarchic order emerged.

The Two Transitions and the Crisis of the System of Oligarchic Domination

Disorder began in the moment of progress. From its very beginning, the prolonged period of stagnation had exposed the inherent weaknesses of an excessively specialized, monoproductive economic structure. By the end of that period, the backwardness of the political system—the so-called oligarchic domination—had also been revealed and discredited. The previous years had been marked by the accumulation of tensions, as solutions to the most pressing social and political problems were postponed, many times by force. The overall level of tensions was only heightened by their latency.

Here it is important to recall that the authoritarian solution—the arbitrary and prolonged monopoly of power—was a procedure imposed from above in order to make the rest of society pay for the oligarchy's temporary salvation. What was initially presented as a short-term response was thereby transformed into a long-term solution, extended by the needs of an unstable balance of forces. This in turn produced a strengthening of the oligarchy's determination to remain intransigent, as is normally the tendency of any class that sees its existence threatened. Mounting social and political calamities, which were direct or indirect consequences of the 1929 depression and the ensuing period of stagnation, eventually affected every level of the social structure.

Sooner or later the course of political history confirms the dictum that the dominated will exchange their freedom for the "protection of the gods," for economic prosperity, order, and harmony. That dictum helps explain the nature of the oligarchic political crisis.

Multiclass coalitions of national dimension, whose leaders did not shy away from the use of direct action, overthrew the military regimes of El Salvador in spring 1944 and of Guatemala in the fall of the same year. A similar coalition also overthrew the civil government of Costa Rica in 1948.[9] Movements of lesser social and political magnitude posed serious challenges to the existing order in both Honduras, from 1945 to 1948, and Nicaragua, where a group of Conservative party youths led by Pedro Joaquín Chamorro provoked a crisis in 1945.

Other analyses have shown quite clearly that the Central American oligarchy first disappeared from the political scene, and only later succumbed economically. This occurred because the challenge to its domination had been set in political terms, elementary though they were.

In the five countries of the isthmus the antioligarchic offensive was shaped by abstract demands for "democracy," a concept then construed as "that which opposed dictatorship." As such, democracy was considered to be more or less synonymous with the right to vote freely. Stimulated by the international climate of the mid-1940s, which had been marked by antifascist victories, popular discontent coalesced for the first time around a specific challenge to the ruling order: the demand for a democratization of the system.

Here it is important to describe the ideological as well as the social nature of this demand in a more precise manner. First of all, the explanation of the backwardness of the political system cannot, in any case, be found in delays produced by the structure of land tenure. Only in Guatemala was there a reformist revolutionary program undertaken that focused on the agrarian structure as the major obstacle to economic development and industrialization.

Rather than as a response to the agrarian structure, then, the goal of democratizing the political system appeared to emerge as a creation of widespread antidictatorial desires. By the end of the 1940s this trend had gained strength and form among university students, professionals, and younger members of the military. It had spread throughout the lower and middle levels of the urban bourgeoisie, helping to shape political parties then forming as substitutes for or competitors to the old two-party system. Their questioning of the oligarchy's authority constituted a threat to the structure of its societal domination. At this early stage the offensive was carried out on an ideological level, guided by progressive intellectuals.

Only Guatemala, from 1951 to 1953, attempted a renovation of its land tenure system. That project of agrarian reform, drawn up jointly by middle class and campesino interests, shook the very foundations of Central American society. It threatened the material bases of oligarchic power through a variety of definitive measures: the expropriation of unproductive estates; the prohibition of servile relationships of any sort; and the declared objectives of diminishing class differences in the countryside while also clearing the way toward independent development. Most alarming of all, however, was the active presence of the campesino masses.

President Jacobo Arbenz's national revolutionary program—which bore no relation to other populist movements of the era—saw two sides to the process of capital accumulation in Guatemala. On the one hand, the agricultural structure itself was considered to be an obstacle; on the other, it was believed that accumulation could be achieved under full national control.

As it turned out, the Program and Praxis of the Arbenz government constituted the zenith of the antioligarchical offensive in Central America. The program not only tested the ideological consistency of the petite bourgeoisie through its criticism of the land tenure system, but also began to shift the initiative for change to the numerically dominant lower classes. Intended as a revolution from above, the Guatemalan experiment soon threatened to spill over into a revolution from below. Or, to use the terminology of that period, it was a bourgeois-democratic

Table 2
Aggregate Value of Agricultural and Manufacturing Production in Central America
($U.S. millions, in real 1970 prices)

	1946*	1955	1960	1965	1970	1976
Agricultural prod.	649.0	980.6	1,167.4	1,525.0	1,839.6	2,384.8
Manufacturing prod.	169.5	338.8	463.8	696.0	991.2	1,407.5

*Data for 1946 are approximate.
Source: *Series Históricas del Crecimiento de América Latina,* ECLA, Santiago,
Chile, 1978, Tables 7 and 9.

revolution bearing the seeds of a possible socialist outcome. The fall of
the government followed soon afterward.[10]

Here it is necessary to introduce a *fourth proposition:* that the political
crisis of the system of oligarchic domination, which had arisen during
the postwar era in the form of a political struggle for democracy and
against dictatorship, was never completely resolved in any Central
American nation. By the time the political crisis occurred—with varying
force in each country—the economic situation was again turning favorable
for the agricultural bourgeoisie and especially for its commercial, coffee-
growing faction. At that time and in a fashion contrary to that which
had occurred fifteen years before—the political crisis was overpowered
by an economic boom.

Here it should be understood that the vitality of the region's agrarian
classes rests with the fate of their primary-exporting sector. That assertion
was effectively confirmed in the 1950s, when the expansion of export
markets enabled that sector to be strengthened and diversified. Nonetheless, that vitality alone does not suffice as a definitive explanation
of the oligarchy's tenacity, though clearly it was a key factor. Coffee
production, for example, tripled between 1945 and 1960, while productivity per acre increased. In addition, the region became the second
largest producer of cotton in the world, and the third largest of meat.
Table 2 is intended as a point of reference to indicate aggregate levels
attained by agricultural and manufacturing production during various
periods.

However, despite these impressive results, a diversity of phenomena,
none of which was necessarily related to any other, contributed to the
permanence of the oligarchic structure. One of those phenomena was
the overthrow of the popular movement in Guatemala. Yet another was
the initiation of industrialization programs at the end of the 1950s; these
took on even greater relevance in the 1960s.

Consequently, a corollary to the fourth proposition can logically be derived from the combined effects of the failure of the antilandowner offensive and the consequent defeat of progressive and popular forces in Guatemala. For when that double failure is considered in conjunction with the successful appearance of advances toward industrialization, certain conclusions can be drawn concerning their likely repercussions on the long-awaited bankruptcy of the oligarchic system of domination. Although some have maintained that those phenomena delayed the political collapse of the old regime, others have claimed that they effectively prevented that collapse.

The corollary to the fourth proposition maintains, therefore, that as a result of those phenomena the most reactionary mode of capitalist development took over throughout the region. Meanwhile the economy, political institutions, and culture of the oligarchic system did not pass on to occupy their proper places in the region's museums of national history. Instead they filtered through every pore of a Central American society in the throes of modernization.

In light of this phenomena it becomes clear that the political crisis of oligarchic domination, which began with the revitalizing winds of the postwar period, was resolved through neither a gradual breakdown nor an abrupt decline of political power. Any possibility of resolution was blocked by the brutal overthrow of the Guatemalan national revolutionary movement in 1954. With the fall of Arbenz, the antioligarchic offensive—in its ideological form as well as its political practice—came suddenly to an end. Similar objectives were to be pursued once again under new programs and methods by the political-military revolutionary movement of the 1970s. But by then, the issue of class struggle would be formulated in different terms.

Once again, what the political crisis could not do, the economy did. Important trends toward economic differentiation facilitated the "metamorphosis" of the backward agrarian bourgeoisie. These trends arose gradually from the reactivation of the export economy, gathering steam in the industrialization project of the 1950s. That process would eventually crystallize as the economic integration program of the 1960s.

What occurred was a gradual and partial modernization of the economic bases of the dominant social structure (which will be discussed later in this chapter under the subtitle "Social Metamorphosis and Economic Growth"). This modernization process took place while the system retained, nonetheless, the most backward "virtues" of oligarchical political practice and leadership. In this metamorphosis, those who are accustomed to a careful reading of history may find ties of kinship between the evolution of the Prussian Junker and that of the conservative bourgeoisie. But here, as in the movies, any resemblance is purely coincidental.

It is now clear that the oligarchic crisis of the postwar years was, in effect, a contradictory transition to a purer bourgeois phase. The period in question was a long one and therefore difficult to summarize. However, the contradictory character of this long transition was not due so much to sluggishness as to the persistence of the ideological and political structure. That structure learned to change its appearance in order to survive.

In reality what we find here are two different transitions—one political, one economic—with different starting times, but eventually occurring simultaneously. They remind one of the storied Chinese bridges that run parallel to one another only to reach different destinations.

In the political sphere, the transition from oligarchic dictatorship to bourgeois democracy led Central American society—with the exception of Costa Rica—to state terrorism and the state of emergency. The political system that emerged was militarized, repressive, and profoundly anti-democratic. In the economic sphere, the transition from a stage of primary-export production to an industrial economy brought the region a semi-industrial, hybrid form of development, which the current crisis has left languishing halfway down the road.

Another corollary can be derived from the fourth proposition (presented earlier) by focusing on the initial, slow process of change, and particularly on the novel elements of that process. These were introduced first by economic and then by political aspects of the transition.

This second corollary suggests, on the one hand, that profound antagonistic contradictions between the agrarian sector and the forces driving industrialization were unnecessary in this period. On the other hand, it maintains that the revolutionary rupture—which occurred as a means of pressing for a less reactionary path of development for Central American society—was hardly inevitable. Today, critical social forces are more readily apparent—due to their unusual vigor—than they were then. However, in the early stages of the transition those forces did not have the opportunity to express themselves.

Finally, the dynamics of growth throughout the entire period cannot be well understood unless an additional factor is included in the analysis. That factor—North American imperialism—was present at all levels of daily life. It took the form of a deep-rooted, internalized force. This imperial policy, it should also be noted, could count on the unflagging support of its regional partners and allies, representatives of the most backward oligarchic groups in each country.

Gone with the Wind?

The oligarchic era in Central America represented, first and foremost, a long period of implanted rural capitalism. More specifically, it meant the passage from a mercantilist economy to dependent capitalism. This transformation was promoted by both favorable processes of socioeconomic development and a particular set of political circumstances. It was a development based on international trade and later supported by direct investment of foreign capital. In both cases, the dynamic impulse came from abroad but interacted with existing local sources of production. Local producers were in turn stimulated and organized by that interaction with foreign commerce.

First came the rise of coffee production, followed by the production of bananas. Until 1950, this situation varied only in quantitative terms. Production curves were always on the rise and critical declines merely served to strengthen the monoproductive cycle.

The creation of an export sector, which eventually became the dynamic foundation of the economy, contributed to a number of important advances in the overall process of nation building. Those tasks included territorial integration, the expansion of state power, the stabilization of political institutions, and the consolidation of the system of domination (consolidation in which the Church also played a central role). For this reason it has been repeated ad nauseum that the formative stage of the oligarchic state corresponded to the period in which coffee became king of the region's economy.

Indeed, in terms of class domination, the process clearly reflected the interests of those factions that had gradually taken control over the newly established sectors of production and commerce. The oligarchy acted, in effect, like a retrograde bourgeoisie, personifying the defects of an agrarian system marked by a subordination of capital accumulation to other interests.

This incomplete predominance of capital arose from imbalances in the structure of land tenure. That structure—based in large estates, parcel plots, and medium-size properties—was supported by the effective submission of the work force and monopolistic control of the early industrialization and commercial processes.

The oligarchic state, and the structures of domination that underlay it, were founded in particular forms of landownership. The oligarchy also depended, therefore, on firm control over the men who worked their lands. Here it should be recognized that in any agrarian economy where the forces of production are poorly developed and levels of capital investment are low, there is one decisive factor in the establishment of the relations of production: control of both the land and its productive potential.

The noncapitalist relations that gradually took root in the Central American coffee plantations (with the exception of Costa Rica, considered further on) were not a result of the "backwardness" of the campesinos, the true producers of the surplus. They were working under conditions of forced labor. To the contrary, that backwardness, as well as the relations of production in which the campesinos reluctantly participated, were a consequence of the general structure of land tenure and the corresponding development of the productive forces.

As is the case in all social relationships, those relations of production implied a relationship of force—of permanently applied extraeconomic violence—in order to maintain them. The oligarchic state, which covers a number of early stages in the process of capital accumulation, was the power entrusted with the task of ensuring the maintenance and generalization of those relations.

It is important to recognize, moreover, that the relations of production in turn determine the relations of distribution. In other words, they shaped the methods by which the oligarchy controlled the social surplus produced by the labor force. The resulting distribution of that surplus— also a by-product of those relations of production—was naturally detrimental to the interests of the majority of the population.

The level of development of the productive forces in the export economy changed both slowly and unevenly. The so-called liberal revolutions made the largest contribution to the development of capitalism in the countryside. Nonetheless, that development remained stunted in the absence of favorable conditions. For a long time in Central America, land, rather than capital, was the fulcrum of social relations. Only recently has the situation changed.

In a similar manner, the separation of the actual producers from the modes of production resulted in a process of "proletarianization" of the campesinos. However, these processes lacked the vigor of the original expansion of capitalism in Europe, a vigor that abstract theory would normally postulate. In any case, the fault lies less with the theory than with the repeated predictions of amateur prophets who anxiously await the transformation of the impoverished into the proletariat.

In a commercial agricultural economy of the sort established in Central America, an economy clearly oriented toward profit, wage labor is not the only form of relationship established between landowner and worker. Indeed the wages that workers receive tend to mask the importance of what is produced on their small private plots, which in turn enables much of the labor force to subsist and to reproduce itself.

The surplus produced on the estate by the workers eventually takes the form of commercial profits. But at an earlier stage, when the product is passed from producer to landowner, that surplus represents a rental payment in kind. Therefore, the coffee baron is little more than a landlord in the traditional sense of the word.

The brief global analysis presented thus far has focused primarily on the bases of the coffee-exporting economy. But similar processes were at work over many years—though operating at different levels—throughout each of the region's national economies. The result was a complex structure of domination, of which the oligarchic state was only a partial manifestation. In any case, the oligarchy has been the only social group or class capable of producing an ideology and of defining a particular vision of the "nation."

Finally, the direct results of those structures that underpinned the oligarchic system also included specific styles of social preeminence and political control. The first of these arose from the parasitic manner in which wealth was accumulated, via rental of land and subordination of the work force. The landlord thereby obtained an excessive degree of power out of all proportion to his financial means. The second of those styles is a necessary consequence of the need to maintain that social preeminence, which can only be achieved through political means. The oligarchy defended the system—including its own class privileges as well as the state itself—using political and ideological mechanisms of control: the restricted vote; sham elections (when they were held); clientelistic party networks at the local level; and a rudimentary form of state power whose legitimation rested ultimately upon self-proclaimed natural rights of leadership.

The oligarchic state, however, had become an outmoded form of bourgeois state attempting to fulfill modern bourgeois tasks. Among those tasks were the pursuit of accumulation in the agrarian sector and the establishment of ties with international capital. The consequent need to politically defend that agrarian wealth and the presence of international capital—as well as the formation of a labor market—produced despotic forms of authority. Oligarchical power in Central America came to be based on a permanent deployment of both legal and physical violence. The result was a police state, constituted as such in order to protect the interests of the dominant class. The democracy of the coffee grower, even considering the differences, resembled Athenian democracy to the degree that it was based on the idea that only land makes men free.

Costa Rica, in this case, was no exception. There, free access to the land did not prevent the consolidation of a more closed, more exclusive, oligarchical structure, founded on the monopoly of commercial and financial capital. Perhaps that explains the Costa Rican oligarchy's relatively progressive character. In any case, the "government of the few," which excluded any possibility of mass participation in politics, was not authoritarian. Public education and religion were used to dress political subordination in decorous liberal pomp.

Elsewhere, as occurred in Nicaragua and Honduras, fights between "notables" added rural despotism to disorder. Guatemala differed from the other countries because of the subordinate position of its ethnic majorities. There a racist vision of society and culture—which served to reinforce that subordination—had become excessive, deep, and permanent. That racial discrimination or pure racism is, in a sense, the morbid expression of oligarchic ideals, a manifestation of conservative ideology befitting lords of the land.[11]

Contrary to what has long been asserted, agrarian classes (note plural) have never been homogeneous. To the contrary, they have responded, in a variety of ways, to the diverse forms of social existence offered by the productive and commercial processes.[12] Their conflicts fill more than a century of history and constitute a fine example of essentially political rivalries. In the Central American case the conflicts revolved around questions that bore no clear relation to an economic base. Rather, they were within a sphere of competition for control of the state.

In summary, the oligarchic state was, without a doubt, a special kind of bourgeois state, marked by peculiar modes of interaction with society. The most important of these was the *separation* between state and society. A distance existed between the two, maintained in order to ensure the continuation of the external conditions of production as well as those of social reproduction.

At the same time, the state showed a strong inclination to defend the interests of the dominant class—to such an extent that the autonomy of the dominant class relative to the state was more or less nonexistent. This took place in the sense that there was an uncontrollable tendency for the "private" (the interests of the dominant agrarian classes) to be confused with the "public," or to appear to be directly involved in specific decisions and actions taken by those in power.

Finally, the forms of legitimation—as well as the values on which that legitimation was based—depended on numerous pillars of support. Among them were a rigid class stratification, the precedence of order over progress, and a submissive, fragmanted citizenry. Naturally, the state constructed upon those pillars was strongly opposed to the interests of the dominated classes.

In short, if politics in bourgeois society is a sphere of activity serving the construction of a social consensus, then the oligarchic state could be considered "prepolitical." Rather than proposing strategies aimed at the incorporation of popular struggles into the political system, the oligarchy continually resorted to the weakest aspect of any system of domination: violence.

Moreover, that oligarchy proved to be incapable of tolerating the appearance of forms of mediation such as the political party or trade union organization. Thus the opportunity to regain some of the region's profound social heterogeneity through bourgeois institutions—institutions responding to popular yearnings for political equality—was bypassed.

The interpretation presented thus far can be summarized in the following manner. In order for capitalism to prosper during a phase in which precapitalist forms of production were being eliminated only very slowly, the oligarchy developed a political and ideological superstructure whose vitality surpassed the lifespan of its economic roots. As the system of domination entered into crisis, during the long transition toward the construction of a more respectable bourgeois society, many of the original characteristics of the political superstructure were lost. Nonetheless, the essential element of that domination persisted: the inability to initiate, extend, and guarantee a truly representative political system. The oligarchy thereby missed the opportunity to build a societal consensus during a period in which Central America had ceased to be little more than a polar composite of landlords and agricultural day laborers.

It was this "heritage," then, that by the end of the postwar period had not yet disappeared, as had the aristocratic heritage of the Old South in *Gone with the Wind*. The postwar period was a time of popular struggles, led by the middle classes, which voiced their demands for a more representative political system and a state that would "govern for all." Their defeat meant the resurgence of policies that turned control and repression into an art form.

Of course the state has not always represented society. That is, it has not always been a place where conflicting class interests could meet and converge in order to form, at least temporarily, a contradictory unity. However, the bourgeois claim to universality confers a generalized national dimension to elite power. That alleged universality is intended to serve the interests of the class that promotes it. The erosion of exclusivist attitudes—in particular the idea that elitist systems of power are a natural phenomenon—does not occur simply in one set of beliefs' disappearance and its replacement by another. Rather, the transformation occurs because extreme levels of force have become necessary in order to maintain the old attitudes.

What was finally shattered over the course of the crisis in Central America was the predominant ideology that had long enlisted the campesinos as natural allies of the agrarian bourgeoisie. That ideology had converted the passivity of the popular masses into the bulwark of bourgeois power, inhibiting the majority of the citizenry from obtaining title to its potential democratic rights. The transformation of those potential demands into action meant the destabilization of the system.

As I shall show in the following pages, Central American society underwent substantial changes during the quarter century following World War II. However, those changes did not bring about, in either a Jacobite or a Prussian sense, the necessary settling of bourgeois accounts vis-à-vis the "ancien regime."

Instead, oligarchical political culture filtered easily through the gaps left by an incomplete process of bourgeois modernization. Moreover, that process was directed primarily from abroad rather than from above and completely disregarded those below. The development of an increasingly bourgeois character of consumption was not paralleled by the development of an equally bourgeois political system.

From the nonexistence of political organizations to their legal prohibition, there existed a critical opportunity that was neither perceived nor tested. In reality, what persisted was "permissible disorganization" backed by the threat of force. Only in Costa Rica was space reserved for subordinate popular organizations—trade unions, peasant leagues, leftist political parties—and for every sort of social-democratic political gamesmanship.

It is now necessary to introduce a *fifth proposition*, which relates directly to the previous point. As already discussed, reformist programs of the democratic political sectors began to appear in the immediate postwar years, headed by professionals and leaders of the middle class. These initiatives have been called the "program of democratic reconstruction and development." The fifth proposition maintains that those initiatives were frustrated, one by one, during the 1960s and early 1970s.

The appearance of a wide spectrum of moderate political forces, with reformist programs and broad popular support, represented an opportune moment for the entire region. The emerging groups advocated, above all, a democratization of the outmoded system of political domination.[13]

Again, Costa Rica managed to sidestep the misfortune of its neighbors. There, from the 1950s on, a sustained attempt at political modernization often preceded the positive development of the economy, in sharp contrast to that which occurred in the rest of the region (see Table 3).

Social Metamorphosis and Economic Growth

Changes in the structure of production over the thirty-year period from 1945 to 1975 had contradictory social effects throughout the region. The complexity of those changes have produced a variety of interpretive analyses. To adopt a zoological perspective of that process, the change

Table 3
Central America: Gross Capital Formation (1950-1968, in \$U.S. millions)

	Costa Rica	Guatemala	Honduras	Nicaragua*
1950	26.90	65.4	28.10	
1951	36.58	70.6	38.00	
1952	45.52	55.6	47.40	
1953	47.57	60.9	48.30	
1954	47.10	60.1	38.45	
1955	54.90	94.0	44.20	
1956	60.82	141.6	46.95	
1957	70.10	153.9	51.95	
1958	58.22	135.2	48.00	
1959	74.54	108.4	47.25	
1960	75.78	107.5	52.40	54.36
1961	82.61	96.0	47.90	57.04
1962	98.87	100.4	60.05	73.94
1963	119.78	133.3	63.30	82.53
1964	91.97	166.6	70.20	104.92
1965	162.18	180.3	80.95	119.43
1966	137.30	149.3	81.65	139.15
1967	149.45	202.8	109.65	137.32
1968	162.65	216.8	115.25	122.29

*Data not available for 1950 to 1959.
Source: Yearbook of National Accounts Statistics, Vol. 2, UN, New York, 1969,
Table 8.

from one thing into another might be compared with the transformation undergone by an animal before reaching its final state of perfection, such as that of a caterpillar emerging from its chrysalis as a butterfly. The oligarchy, then, *metamorphosed* into bourgeoisie. In order to offer a theological explanation, one might turn to the term *metempsychosis,* which refers to the transmigration of the soul of a dead person to another living thing. In this sense, the defunct oligarchy revived itself in a bourgeois body. It is worthwhile analyzing that transformation.

In the thirty years following the end of World War II, Central American economic development experienced a sustained cycle of expansion and stagnation, of boom and bust. The political characteristics of that cycle posed limits to the process of social differentiation and to the emergence of a new capitalist class structure.

But we must carefully examine whether the hypothesis contained in the fourth proposition is plausible within the framework of the preceding explanation. Implicit in that hypothesis was the assumption that the oligarchy saved itself as a class through partial modifications of its political and social role. These modifications took place within the context of an economy marked by renewed capitalist growth in the agrarian sector and the establishment of an industrial base by the early 1960s.

Here it should be remembered that the production of primary goods for the international market does not, in itself, necessarily constitute an insuperable hurdle on the road to local industrial development. Neither history nor theory would indicate such a hypothesis.

However, the agro-export economy is not exactly an ideal incubator of industrial growth. Internal and external factors can favor or limit that growth. In the history of Central American underdevelopment, capital penetrated the countryside in the form of mercantile capital, taking control of lines of production that were supported to a greater or lesser extent by precapitalist forms of production and social relations.

In the same way as occurred elsewhere, however, capitalism did not develop within the agricultural sector itself. Rather, it evolved in other sectors—such as commerce, finance, and manufacturing—affecting agriculture largely from without. The development of the internal productive forces was therefore weak. So-called agrarian capitalism did not encompass the entire sector, nor was it characterized by social relations based on free wage labor.

In the dualist vision of society, a structural separation exists between the modern export sector and the rest of the economy. The latter, the backward part of the economy, is in turn divided between artisan and subsistence sectors. But what occurred in Central America was a total subordination of the backward sectors to the modern one. The whole of society was marked by the fate of its primary exports, which were both the basis and the result of the oligarchic period. With the modernization of production, the agricultural sector became even more heterogeneous. There it was not the product that defined the producer, but rather the reverse.

The modernization of the agricultural sector did not begin until the early 1950s, and then was only partial. This modernization occurred as the local industrial sector was forming and access to new foreign technical innovations became relatively easier. The process was initially slowed because of the dominance of coffee, a crop with limited potential to benefit from the advances of modern technology. But the region's other major postwar export commodities—sugarcane, cotton, bananas, and beef—were significantly affected by the modernization of production techniques. Though hardly an "agrarian revolution," as bureaucratic terminology would claim, that modernization was certainly a decisive factor in the renovation of the primary sector.

It was, nonetheless, a stifled modernization, because rather than covering the whole of the agricultural economy, only a part of the export sector was included. Moreover, production of food crops for the domestic

Table 4
Central America: Growth Rates in Production, Employment and Productivity
(1960-1971, annual average, in real 1961 prices)

	1 Growth of Value-added	2 Growth of Employment	3 Growth of Productivity (1-2)
Primary sector	4.8	1.9	2.9
Secondary sector	7.2	4.2	3.0
Tertiary sector	5.3	3.5	1.8
Total GDP	5.6	2.7	2.9

Source: Clark W. Reynolds, "Fissures in the Volcano? Central American Economic Prospects," in J. Grunwald (ed.), *Latin America and the World Economy: A Changing International Order,* Sage Publications, Beverly Hills, Calif., 1978, p. 202. Reprinted by permission.

market—rice, beans, corn, vegetables, and fruits—regressed in relative as well as absolute terms.[14] Having been reduced to small private plots, the production of basic grains was more or less paralyzed. Food production, incapable of assimilating new technology and capital investment, slid into a pattern of recurring shortfall.

As a result, it was not contradictory to find a dynamic coffee sector—with ever-greater control over all stages of the production and commercialization processes—existing side by side with traditional landowners who continued to use old-fashioned production methods. At the same time, urban and foreign sources were providing capital to be invested in the expansion of cotton, sugar cane, and beef production. That capital originated in the form of either public credit or direct foreign investment.[15]

There is a familiar statistical indicator of the changes that took place in the structure of production during the period being examined. Although the indicator's value is only relative, it nonetheless has no substitute: an average annual growth rate of 5.4 percent of the gross domestic product (GDP) over a period of twenty-five years. That of course is even greater than the dizzying rate of population growth for the same period.

Though the growth of the industrial sector was yet faster than that of the agricultural sector (see Tables 4 and 5), the latter still contributed 26 percent of GDP and employed 60 percent of the economically active population. Agricultural commodities also accounted for 80 percent of extraregional exports.[16]

Table 5
Central America: Indicators of Economic Growth

	1960	1970	1980	1987
Industrial value-added (v.-a.)*	1,387	3,088	5,134	5,158
Growth rate of v.-a. in industrial sector**		8.3	5.2	0.1
Agricultural value-added*	2,976	4,777	6,586	6,635
Growth rate of v.-a. in agricultural sector**		4.8	3.3	0.1
Percentage GDP/manufacturing	13.5	17.1	18.4	18.2
Percentage GDP/agriculture	29.0	26.5	23.5	23.4
Acquired public debt balance***	203	883	8,320	17,418
Gross domestic investment*	1,414	2,752	4,715	4,034
Growth rate of gross domestic investment**		6.9	5.5	-2.2

*In $U.S. millions, 1986.
**Average annual rates.
***In $U.S. millions, current.
Source: *Progreso Económico y social de América Latina,* FLACSO's data archives, based on BID, Washington, D.C. Various years.

In 1980, aggregate production of the region's industrial sector was valued at $3.6 billion, while agricultural production reached $4.7 billion. The so-called industrialization level rose to 19.1 percent of GDP. Compared with the 11.5 percent of the mid-1950s, that level indicates unquestionable qualitative change. The industrialization level of Latin America as a whole was not inordinately higher, with a 1980 figure of 25.6 percent.

In any case, the Central American industrializatiion did not derive its dynamism from commercial agrarian accumulation, as one might have supposed. When industrialization gradually began to take form, at the end of the 1950s, two factors guided its development. One was the weight of foreign capital and technology, coming from abroad. The other—internal—was active promotion by the state.

The package of protective measures that eventually emerged was designed to establish a regional industrial haven. The poorly named Central American Common Market—in reality a zone opened almost completely to free trade—was an explicit attempt on the part of the state to reconcile agrarian and industrial interests. Rather than vertically expanding domestic markets in order to increase local consumption, a single horizontal market was created. That political substitute meant little more than the geographical amplification of limited demand. That demand had of course been stimulated by the boom period of the 1950s but had been sorely neglected during the long period of stagnation from 1930 to 1945.

The "nonagression pact" finally arrived at between sectoral interests consequently left the traditional system of land tenure intact, transfering the oligarchy's fate to the laws of the market. Those laws, in the course of a generation, would accomplish what politics could not. The social pact, in effect, overcame a false conflict of interests. It was successful in Central America because the dominant classes of the five countries were closely related to one another. Though of course differing from sector to sector, those classes shared an agricultural income base that they were loath to give up. At the same time, however, they shared an ever-growing dependency on industrial and commercial profit.

The bourgeois transformation of the dominant agrarian commercial classes depended on variations in the degree of national control over the extended lines of production. But here there arose a fundamental distortion in the mechanisms of accumulation, as the structure of production entered into contradiction with the conditions under which commodities were being produced.

In the case of the national coffee sector, for example, the owners of the production ventures themselves only partially controlled the final value of the product. That disadvantageous situation originated with the intermediation of international commercial and financial capital— first English, then North American—and was further affected by the nature of external demand. Neither the level of prices nor that of demand depended on local costs or productivity. Rather, they both responded to cyclical variations in the international market.

Capitalist development was characterized, until the middle of this century, by the way in which the functional subordination of precapitalist methods of agricultural production was exploited as the principal mechanism of accumulation. The appropriation of the surplus value occurred not only via the extraction of surplus labor from the campesinos, but also through control of the semi-industrial processing of coffee. The changes that have been examined throughout this chapter tended to destroy the most backward methods of surplus value extraction. Social divisions deepened within the agricultural work force[17] as the expansion of wage labor and mechanization were incorporated into the relations of production.

The oligarchy in its classic conception—a historical actor that seized others' lands and exploited a semiservile work force—no longer exists in Central America. Economic differentiation as well as protective state policies created conditions that enabled a modern agrarian bourgeoisie to arise in its place. Landowner-capitalists became capitalist-landowners. This did not signify the destruction of the class but rather its decomposition. In other words, it meant the collapse of the most backward social groups and the appearance of new bourgeois sectors.

The appearance of large capital enterprises in the production of coffee, cotton, sugar, and meat was a process common to each of the nations of Central America. However, the extent to which that process took place varied among the five. One important difference was the degree to which changes occurred with respect to the class structure. In addition, some countries were more able than others to take advantage of their respective—and unequal—opportunities for modernization. Those differences grew out of processes that concentrated and centralized capital over the 1945–1975 period. The result was the formation of a dominant *grande bourgeoisie* based in the agro-export sector. It was a class characterized by monopolistic control over the decisive phases of agricultural production.

This process was most advanced in Costa Rica, though not only because favorable economic foundations already existed there. Costa Rica's advance was also due to state efforts,[18] which since 1950 had been explicit, consistent, and sustained. Together with the old oligarchy— increasingly modernized—state policies created new bourgeois sectors tied to agricultural production. That was, perhaps, the decisive accomplishment of the Costa Rican path toward development.

The experience of agrarian classes in Guatemala and El Salvador was different. In those countries the oligarchy adopted certain bourgeois traits without abandoning its long tradition of land accumulation.[19] The concentration of agro-industrial capital was based on a monopoly over control of the land. Once again, a group of families took charge of all investment opportunities.

The high level of land concentration and monopoly in pre-Sandinista Nicaragua was revealed via the expropriation of rural properties belonging to the Somoza Group.[20] Once the total output of those lands had been calculated, the revolutionary state realized that it had inherited some 40 percent of the nation's agricultural production.

In brief, with a few differences of tone in various countries that did not alter the generally limited nature of the class recomposition, the economic diversification of the old oligarchy gave way to a modern agro-exporting bourgeoisie. However, the new bourgeoisie did not define itself merely in terms of its new means of economic existence. Rather, its activities began to expand into a variety of entrepreneurial ventures. With investments in industry, commerce, and finance, the old limits were definitively abandoned. Actually the process worked both ways, because commercial-financial capital investments were equally important to agricultural enterprises.

This process of functional diversification of large economic groups—of both old and new vintage—was possible in Central America for the following reasons:

1. The demographic and social dimensions of national and regional markets limited their potential for diversified production.
2. The unequal distribution of wealth—initially based on land, but later including other forms of social wealth—created an extreme concentration of income.
3. The industrialization process was controlled by North American capital and protected by the state.

The transfer of capital goods and managerial techniques also took place under favorable political conditions, further facilitating the relocation of commercial and agrarian capital. Therefore, a prolonged, painful process of bourgeois revolution had not been necessary in order to convince elite coffee growers where there true interests lay. The well-advised responded by purchasing shares of stock in industry and by opening their bank accounts for use as industrial credit.[21]

Two basic factors, then, explain the absence of turmoil between landowners and industrialists in Central America. One was the multi-sectoral nature of the bourgeoisie. The other was an unusual brand of capitalism both promoted and managed politically. At the same time, these factors contribute to an explanation of the ensuing interbourgeois conflict, which constitutes one of the most characteristic elements of the current political crisis.

Central America at the Crossroads

In the 1970s a wide spectrum of economic, social, and political factors converged in an essentially *national* sense. Those factors—both regional and international—were of diverse origin and significance. Over the course of the decade, the dynamism that had propelled Central American economic growth to a degree previously unknown in the region[22] began to wane. The strong cooperative trends that had produced regional economic integration lost momentum.

Industrial growth, of course, had not been the sole factor behind the region's heroic episode of dependent capitalism in the 1960s. Intraregional trade, the high value of traditional and nontraditional products, and the volume of foreign investment had also played key roles throughout the period.

Furthermore, it was not the appropriately named "useless war" between El Salvador and Honduras in 1969 that broke the commercial and productive optimism of the Central American Common Market (CACM). Imbalances were implicit in the way foreign capital had seized control of the bourgeois-nationalist program. In its struggle to achieve balanced regional industrial growth, that program had sought to grant the principal role in the process to the state, rather than the private sector.

When the twentieth anniversary of the signing of the CACM's General Treaty of Economic Integration was celebrated in June 1981, it was evident that the event's symbolic breaking of porcelain ware was also symbolic of the fragility of the program. That weakness was not due so much to the presence of large foreign multinational firms as to the freedom with which they operated.

The CACM's crisis, which emerged after 1971, primarily took the form of a declining volume of intraregional trade. That decline resulted from each government's need to defend the interests of its private sector. Conflicts that surfaced were interbourgeois conflicts disguised as national struggles. At the same time, the principal regional organizations proved to be impotent in their attempts to confront the situation, though they themselves were unaware of their weakness. Actually, fundamental imbalances favoring Guatemalan and Salvadoran enterprises were at the heart of the crisis.

The nature of the crisis was also affected by another by-product of capitalist growth. With the sudden acceleration of that growth during the 1960s, both the concentration of income and structural unemployment (absolute as well as relative) increased considerably. However, the transitory expansion only timidly obscured what emerged after 1971 as an indecent exhibition of poverty and rebellion.

In the early 1970s, soon after the CACM began to crumble, international capitalism entered a second phase of its critical cycle. Its internal effects bore only a superficial resemblance to those of the 1929–1930 crisis. Essentially what occurred was a decline in international demand, which in turn produced falling prices for the region's primary-export commodities and corresponding losses of national income.

By then, however, Central American society was no longer connected to the foreign market strictly through commercial ties. A more complex and binding relationship had united the region with the developed economies. At the international level, new forms of dependency became manifest with increases in the cost of imported energy and capital in general. At the national level, increasing demand for capital goods and semifinished products for local industry as well as the luxurious tastes of high-income minority groups made the economy only more vulnerable. The nature of the region's dependency had become at once more modern and more catastrophic.

Due to rising costs of petroleum, inflation began to hit the region as of 1973. It would be difficult—and also unnecessary—to specify what percentage of the inflation was imported from abroad and what percentage should be attributed to local structural causes. More important is to consider its consequences. Indeed, the rise in prices was so general that even corn—a basic nutrient that had never before been subjected to the laws of capital—was affected. The popular masses learned—through harsh experience—that inflation is a disease that strikes the poor more severely than the rich, that it is a clearly malignant means of capital accumulation.

The initial lack of a popular response was partly due to the fact that Central America had never suffered the hardships of real inflation. Moreover, no organized channels existed that could serve as conduits of the protest stimulated by that phenomenon. These factors must be kept in mind when analyzing the regional crisis.

For the bulk of Central American society, the brief and artificial stimulation that occurred between 1975 and 1977 had repercussions much like those of an injection of a narcotic for a drug addict. One chronic problem was the foreign debt[23] accompanied by recurrent negative trade balances and uninterrupted fiscal crisis.

From 1979 on, stagnation was followed by regression in the agricultural sector, further feeding the current account deficits. Between 1979 and 1980 three countries—Costa Rica, Nicaragua, and El Salvador—registered negative growth rates. In 1981 Guatemala joined the club of invalids.

The new period of international disorder produced effects within those countries that are as yet only poorly understood. Those effects originated in dependent economies marked, on the one hand, by high degrees of openness to external influences, and on the other, by a lack of effective state protection. The Central American state's only real concern was the maintenance of domestic political order.

We return now to the essay's initial concern. It would be totally incorrect to deduce from the preceding discussion that the political class struggle for state power was nothing more than a veiled reflection of the region's economic imbalances. The interpretation is not exact. This is clearly illustrated by the divergent cases of Costa Rica, on the one hand, and Guatemala, El Salvador, and Nicaragua (before 1979), on the other.

Regional struggles have revolved around exploitation—that is, the contradictions between capital and labor—and the reproduction of social relations. Differences in those struggles from one nation to another are at the root of those divergences. The popular masses have gradually organized themselves into armed movements, constituting challenges to the entire social structure. It is clear that they are fighting for more than wage increases and protection from inflation. It is here that the political system regains its relative autonomy and that the phenomena themselves become critical factors. Therefore, those phenomena need to be explained in order to clarify the true dimensions of the economic crisis.

The "interaction" of those dimensions is a strictly national affair, deriving from past history. The contemporary aspects of the national crises in Central America can only be explained by analyses of the national class struggles as they develop. This entails a comprehensive examination of both subjective factors—the successive failures of protest actions followed by renewed desire to see them triumph—and objective determinations of changing structural configurations. The latter implies an interpretation not only of industrial and agrarian capitalism as well as its social effects, but also of the bourgeoisie, of both its material and ideological power.

It was during the 1970s that a complex convergence of internal and external factors critically affected the entire sphere of social relations throughout the region. Those factors had impact on the system of material reproduction as much as on political-ideological mechanisms governing order in society. It is not possible here to make a detailed analysis of each element constituting the "eruption" that shook Guatemala and El

Salvador in particular, nor those that acted upon Nicaragua and have threatened to do the same in Honduras.[24]

The outstanding feature of this process, however, is the autonomous irruption of the popular masses—especially the campesinos—who burst onto the political scene via new forms of organization. This occurred in areas where politics had never been "practiced" before. Extremely violent methods of struggle were used in the struggle against the permanently repressive nature of bourgeois domination. The irruption revealed that the capitalism typical of backward societies, characterized by the polarization that often marks class conflict and by the lack of normal channels capable of absorbing social conflict, was vulnerable.

The organized protests of the subordinated classes occurred simultaneously with a growing loss of political control, a repeated lack of hegemonic leadership. That relative weakening of the elite grip on society meant an almost permanent refusal to seek a social consensus that would support its class domination.

Here an essential feature of oligarchic domination appears: It was incapable of entrusting the state with representative powers in a national dialogue, of establishing or profiting from political mediation. As a result, assaults against the "superstructure" became inevitable, and any offensive mounted by the dominated classes was bound to be relatively strong.

In order to bring this chapter to a close, I shall offer a *final proposition*. That proposition asserts that the political crisis—experienced by the entire region as a profound rupture affecting the totality of social relations—was the unified expression of two critical processes. One of those processes was the old oligarchic crisis, which remained unresolved through bourgeois renovation. The other was a crisis of the capitalist order in general, produced by the various forms of struggle for popular participation as well as by the state's response to those movements.

Both crises became confused and intertwined as the general crisis took on an increasingly political form, because it was at the political level that the underlying class contradictions presented themselves. In effect, the virulence of the conflict and the speed with which the state order crumbled resulted in a prima facie questioning of the state's role as regulator and leader of society.

The current political crisis is a manifestation of the state's generalized disorganization. As a consequence, that crisis is viewed as a challenge to the entire system, testing the resilience of all social forces. The result is an epic struggle where victory means the domination of one class over another, and where violence and state terrorism play major supporting roles.

The final stage of the oligarchic crisis arose because the agrarian economy was never fully modernized nor replaced by a solid industrial economy. A peaceful coexistence was established, achieved through a process of gradual transition, which prolonged the existence of the most backward part of the agrarian sector. The foundations of that sector remained the monopoly of landownership and the persistence of a rural contradiction that capitalism never resolved: that of campesinos subjected to a continually postponed social decomposition that only impoverished them more from year to year.

Meanwhile within the dominant structure the most backward sectors—the remnants of the oligarchy—were still present, endowed with that final lucidity which precedes one's own demise. It was they who advocated the defense of private landownership as if it were the system's last stand. In the face of oligarchical fears of death, internal ruptures within the bourgeoisie appear to have been forgotten.

The crisis of the system itself has been hypothesized as a derivation from the preceding processes. The antioligarchical struggle that ensued, nevertheless, maintained a political and ideological nature. Meanwhile the bourgeois contradiction evolved in the economic field, where the bourgeoisie was the decisive element. In this intertwining of the two crises it is evident that political domination and state power tended to express an oligarchic rather than a bourgeois character. Methods of control were marked by the repressive, antidemocratic policies of the previous period. But there was no confusion of tasks. The shadow of the oligarchy continued to project its image onto the illuminated plane of class struggle.

What happened, then, is that the crisis that confronted the oligarchy was obliged to evolve into a struggle against the bourgeoisie. The interbourgeois conflict was overpowered by the surging anti–status quo dynamic of the popular offensive. The armed popular forces modified their former programs and battlefronts, converting themselves into truly national, anticapitalist movements.

With the fall of the Somoza dictatorship, the popular offensive moved on to confront anticapitalist tasks. The final battle against the oligarchy took place July 19, 1979. What followed was the collapse of the system.

For that reason it is hardly coincidental that in El Salvador—in order to neutralize a popular offensive on the verge of triumph—an agrarian reform was enacted and banks and foreign trade were nationalized. Those decisions represented three blows to the very heart of the agrarian classes.

Thus the winding path of the crisis now finds Central America at a crossroads. But it is difficult to imagine a solution that could manage to separate the most backward dominant sectors from those that form the modern bourgeois order. This, then, leads to an extensive questioning of that bourgeoisie's societal hegemony and of the power apparatus in which that class—with clear complicity—has participated.

Notes

1. Nicos Poulantzas, *Fascismo y Dictadura* (Siglo Veintiuno Editores, Mexico City, 1971), p. 58.

2. Ruy Mauro Marini, *El Reformismo y la Contrarrevolución* (Série Popular ERA 37, Mexico City, 1976), pp. 92–94. Marini uses this distinction in order to explain how, in the Chilean case, the conquest of the state apparatus did not resolve the question of power.

3. See Chapter 4. For the original Spanish version see "Ocho claves para comprender la crisis política de Centroamérica," in *Polémica*, No. 1, San José, Costa Rica, 1981. That previous work developed these aspects of the crisis in only a tangential manner. Obviously, to advance the understanding of the Central American crisis, the analysis of major actors and the manner in which they interact is insufficient without an examination of the stage upon which they move.

4. The point here is not to indicate what could have been an appropriate economic policy. The need for a fiscal policy designed to mitigate the effects of the crisis is less, for example, in societies such as those of this period in Central America, than in industrialized countries—where unemployment affects a considerable proportion of the population and where those who are victimized generally live exclusively from wage income. In Central America the number of industrial workers has been small compared to the size of the agricultural population, which in general, in this earlier period, was not adversely affected by cyclical fluctuations. The well-being of those living in the countryside depends, basically, on their levels of basic crop production. What misery and malaise occurred were primarily a result of the unnecessarily long duration of the depressed period.

5. By restricting the data to the production and export of coffee, as an indicator of the overall behavior of the economy, I have clearly abused accepted methodological standards of sociohistorical analysis. However, during this era, coffee alone represented 40 percent of the region's gross domestic product and constituted the dynamic core of its economy. The effects of World War II were similar to those of the crisis of 1929–1930, once again paralyzing exports more than production. A more rigorous analysis of the data would not merely use the word stagnation, but rather would refer to oscillations, specifying the declines of 1929–1932 and 1940–1944 experienced throughout the region.

6. Surpluses and deficits in the commercial balance of a monoexporting economy can have contradictory effects on the ordered growth of a society of this sort. At that time in Central America the surpluses and deficits did not cause significant inflationary pressures. Through analysis of a longer period than that under consideration, however, it becomes evident that no fiscal policy capable of "curing" a depression originating abroad existed. Nor could any policy have

limited the distortions caused by a "boom" in exports produced by a rise in prices rather than an increase in productivity.

7. Once again, in highly specialized primary-exporting economies, fiscal revenues were particularly sensitive to fluctuations in national income. The imbalanced economic structure generated serious malfunctions within the state apparatus, as a drastic decline in public income occurred. The spending cuts that followed made the idea of policies such as public works, government purchase of harvested crops, and expansion of credit unimaginable. For example, in Guatemala, the revenues of fiscal year 1928–1929 ($15.3 million) were not equaled until 1945. In 1939 the Salvadoran state collected $8.5 million, a figure not achieved again until 1944. For further discussion of these problems, see Henry Wallich and James Adler, *Proyecciones Económicas de las Finanzas Públicas: un estudio experimental en El Salvador,* and James Adler et al., *Las Finanzas Públicas y el desarrollo económico de Guatemala,* FCE, Mexico City, 1949 and 1952, respectively.

8. The form in which agrarian capital reproduced itself and accumulated was the same as that which had taken place since the beginning of the century. It was a question of how to move more rapidly down paths that were already being followed, but too slowly: extension of cultivated lands; superexploitation of the work force; a labor market based on the *mozo colono* (see note 17); and sharecropping. To sum up, the goal was the extraction of an extraordinary income in order to build a base of surplus value that could then be divided between local producer profits and funds directed to foreign commercial and finance capital.

9. The short civil war of 1948 and the intense periods of violence that preceded it constituted symptoms of a political crisis of extraordinary scope, marked by an unusual mix of class interests. Costa Rica was unable to escape the highly significant wave of political class struggle that rose throughout the region, although the process assumed particular characteristics there. What occurred in 1948 constitutes, without a doubt, the confrontation between two bourgeois factions. One sought to change—the other to maintain—the social bases of the political system. A complex system of alliances makes the analysis all the more difficult. One faction allied itself with the Communist party and the Catholic church. The other, equally representative of the coffee-growing oligarchy, took sides with progressive sectors of the middle classes. Costa Rican historians have devoted the bulk of their efforts to an analysis of the strange marriage between Conservative President Rafael Calderón Guardia, the Partido Vanguardia Popular (Communist party), and the Catholic church, led by Archbishop Victor Manuel Sanabria. Little, however, has been done in terms of examining the fragility of the anti-Calderón alliance.

10. As the intention here is not to analyze the causes of the Guatemalan popular movement of 1954, the event is merely mentioned. There now exists a rather considerable number of works available on the subject, though a more profound analysis would be most welcome.

11. Some scholars have qualified the oligarchic state as a neocolonial one, because it is incapable of establishing the necessary conditions to achieve national

and social integration. It seems unnecessary to resort to the imprecision of this concept, however, which can easily be illustrated by returning to the European birthplace of capitalism, where the subordinate classes were integrated in a gradual and most uneven manner.

12. The landholders appear here not merely as owners of the coffee plantations. They were also the bourgeoisie of the local store, in control of all sources of credit capital. Finally, they included the small group that monopolized the agro-industrial process as well as various channels of profit and commercialization that eventually led to foreign markets.

13. The forces that promoted what I have called the "project of democratic reconstitution with development" were in general weak and emerged at different times. Moderate forces in Guatemala attempted a comeback in 1963 via the election of Juan José Arévalo; in El Salvador there was the election of José Napoleon Duarte in 1972; and in Nicaragua a substitute for Somoza in the wake of the 1972–1973 Liberal-Conservative pact could have been the opportunity for an ordered, reformist succession. In each case the army, with the agreement of North American policymakers, negated such solutions. It is not mere coincidence that in each of those countries the first outbreaks of popular armed insurgency occurred following the frustration of democratic, developmentalist projects and the disillusionment of those projects' leaders.

14. Some exceptions must be noted. In Costa Rica and Nicaragua, for example, rice was cultivated in modern enterprises, employing capital-intensive techniques. The same was true of Guatemalan wheat, which was produced on moderately mechanized small- and medium-size farms. But corn remained the most important product and was produced under the worst economic conditions.

15. In 1976, Central America exported the following percentages of Latin American products: 22 percent of coffee, 42 percent of cotton, 58 percent of bananas, and 30 percent of meat. See ECLA, *Centroamérica, evolución económica desde la post-guerra* (ECLA/Mex/ODE/34, Mexico City, 1979), Table 20.

16. A paradox of Central America is that economic growth depends on the agricultural sector, whereas rural development itself constitutes an obstacle to attaining higher industrial levels.

17. The *mozo colono* was tied to the land, his small plot serving as part of his "salary." That form of labor has essentially disappeared, replaced by a paid, agrarian semiproletariat. Moreover, the domestic market for wage goods has expanded, and the new structure of domestic financing is completely different from the former one. In any case it would be difficult, in this chapter, to empirically verify the degree to which the methods of domestic capital accumulation have adopted the new mechanisms.

18. The economic policies of the Partido Liberación Nacional (social-democratic sui generis) were to a large extent the inspirational force behind this project of agrarian capitalist modernization. The fundamental difference between that project and those of other societies in the region was of a political nature. The process of social differentiation, stimulated by the state, was brought about through democratic procedures. The social and political costs were therefore relatively low.

19. For example, in 1971, 6 families (Guirola, Sol, Dueñas, Daglio, Samayoa, and Romero Bosque) owned 71,923 hectares of land, or the same amount as about 132,000 campesino owners of small private plots. In 1974, 62 percent of exported coffee was sold by 10 families, while 228,000 tons of sugar were produced by the Regalado and Bustamante families alone. See Eduardo Colindres, "La tenencia de la tierra en El Salvador," *ECA*, No. 335/336, 1976, p. 471. In Guatemala, Raúl García Granados emerged in 1973 as Latin America's largest cotton producer, with a total of about 14,000 tons. Meanwhile, three coffee enterprises processed 40 percent of Guatemala's exportable production.

20. Until 1979, three such groups existed in Nicaragua: the Banic Group (Liberal party capital), the Banamérica Group (Conservative party capital), and the Somoza Group—the latter of which was the most powerful.

21. See Edelberto Torres-Rivas, "Naturaleza y Crisis del Poder en Centroamérica," *Estudios sociales centroamericanos*, No. 3, Costa Rica, 1973, p. 46.

22. Between 1961 and 1970 regional industrial output grew at an annual rate of 8.6 percent in real 1980 dollars. Rates for Nicaragua and Costa Rica exceeded 11 percent. For the same period, the overall Latin American rate was 6.5 percent.

23. Industrial growth was not completely financed by private domestic savings. Other sources such as international capital and foreign loans filled the gaps, producing mounting debts. Public foreign debt in 1977 was thirty-five times that of 1960. By 1970, Central America expended $92 million in total debt service payments. By 1979 it was paying $625.8 million; that is to say, about seven times more.

24. This subject matter has been partially dealt with in Chapter 4.

3

Who Took the Lid Off Pandora's Box? Reflections on the Crisis in Central America

. . . but the gods took revenge on man, sending to Earth a woman endowed with all seductive charms—Pandora—whom Epimetheus was imprudent enough to marry. For Pandora possessed a box, from which all forms of evil escaped, scattering themselves throughout the land. Who was to blame, Pandora or Prometheus' brother? Only Hope remained, caught beneath the edges of the box, for the consolation of man.

—from Greek mythology

The Crisis Did Not Begin Yesterday

Central American society entered a critical period in the middle of the 1970s. However, the roots of that crisis—whose effects were most severe in Nicaragua, Guatemala, and El Salvador—are of differing lengths, extending well back into the region's history. It is difficult to give exact dates as to when those historic processes began, for the crisis they produced was only recognizable once its effects had become apparent. The development of that crisis in turn impinged on relations between social classes, turning those relations ever more confrontational until they had reached their contemporary expression of extreme violence.

Conflict arose at the political level in Central America and bore two easily verified characteristics: First, it rapidly altered social relations, which had traditionally served to assure authority or control over the

45

vast majority of the population; and second—in the wake of that rupture—the popular response became organized in political-military terms as armed resistance.

The antecedents to that two-sided result, at the regional as well as local level, have been analyzed with mixed success. In some cases, the crisis has been presented as having political origins, as the consequence of either the possibility of or the denial of democratic practice. In that perspective, political failure occurred because the political system never achieved a democratic, liberal and bourgeois consistency. Seen in this vein, the crisis appears to be the radical failure of an ideal order, the failure of a program that sought the integration of all classes into the political system.

In other cases, the structure of the dependent capitalist order has been the focus of analysis. Here the obstacles are considered to be economic, posed by a poorly functioning capitalism whose development process generated insuperable problems. In this perspective, the crisis was the failure of a productive system that did not achieve the integration of all classes into the market. In any case, these partial explanations have left unanswered the fundamental question of why those failures occurred.

For Central America the reductionist interpretation also proves to be inadequate because, during the postwar era, there was significant economic growth, with considerable social differentiation. At the same time, the state was growing, expanding its functions as its internal structure became more complex. In sum, the whole of society changed, and any attempt to explain the crisis must be based upon those changes, upon their ultimate nature.

In the 1970s two critical processes dating from different times concurred and were united in the disruptive action of the popular masses. The latter were thereby converted from passive objects into active subjects of the conflict, into a force capable of defining its interests in terms of political power. The last section of this chapter will return to a consideration of the character of those subjects of the crisis and to the revolutionary, popular dimension of their movement.

For the time being, however, the focus will be on the two critical processes mentioned above. First of all, there has been the oligarchic crisis, which is of an essentially political nature despite the role it inevitably plays in any criticism of the primary-export economic order.

The emergence of popular and democratic struggles, which first occurred toward the end of World War II, represented a radical challenge not only to the coffee growers' state, but also to the entire system of domination, whose roots stretched back to the middle of the nineteenth century. The solution to that crisis was postponed time and time again, the democratic road repeatedly not taken. That political paralysis prevented a bourgeois renovation of the traditional order and the creation of a state truly representative of the nation.

More recently, but closely tied to that oligarachic crisis, there has also occurred what might be called the crisis of the bourgeois order. But here there has no longer been any attempt to modify that bourgeois order, as had been the case during the period of the antioligarchic offensive. Rather, the opposition's goal became the ousting and destruction of the bourgeoisie. The existence of armed popular masses, with anticapitalist programs, has left little room for doubt about those objectives.

What we are dealing with, then, is a single crisis, regardless of how many allusions are made—within a framework of extreme social, economic, and cultural heterogeneity—to a crisis in the pattern of development, accompanied by a crisis in the model of hegemony, and fed by a series of easily retraced historical events.

Some of those events originated in the heart of an agrarian society that is export oriented and campesino based; others arose in an urban society, industrial and primarily worker based. Structural causes, then—with "structure" understood as the organizational nature and dynamic of the society's productive system[1]—lie at the center of the analysis. There are also external factors that contribute to the internal dynamic of the Central American crisis, but they will be left aside temporarily due to the priorities of the present analysis.

It is important to discuss briefly what is meant by the term *oligarchy*. Certainly it involves a theoretical social category, and the term as such is often used in a contradictory, equivocal way within the social sciences. In this analysis, the oligarchical era in Central American society comprises the long period of the implantation of rural capitalism, of the establishment of commercial-export enterprises (principally coffee), and of the linkage of local production to international capital. By the end of the nineteenth century, the export sector had become the dynamic pole of the "national" economy, which therefore took on a notably external orientation.

That dynamism also contributed to the slow and partial fulfillment of various national objectives, such as the gradual solidification of state power and the stability of the state's physical apparatus: the political institutions that generated and expressed class authority. That dynamism, in other words, favored the relative consolidation of a system of domination based upon the predominance of the few in conjunction with the fundamental exclusion of the majority.

The Central American "oligarchy," therefore—as a (fraction of a) class—was the result of a backward process of bourgeois social change, a personification of the incomplete predominance of capital in agrarian production and in the commercialization of foreign trade. That production was based on a system that included large landed estates as well as campesino-managed parcel plots in their various forms. It was built upon both the formal submission of the work force and monopolistic control—by an elite composed largely of foreign owners and recent arrivals—over various stages of the production process, particularly, processing and foreign trade.[2]

A certain confusion inevitably arises from the fact that no oligarchic state or society actually exists. This confusion demands clarification. The adjective *oligarchical*—a highly contradictory term—refers to the kind of power that made the original accumulation process possible. That power facilitated the concentration of agrarian wealth under monopolistic conditions and also ensured—via mechanisms that frequently violated traditional codes of valor—the maintenance and reproduction of a society based on violent extraction of the social surplus produced by campesino and semiproletarian, working-class labor.

In addition, "oligarchical" domination implied a particular brand of political behavior practiced by the dominant groups. That behavior was the expression of an all-encompassing social and cultural predominance that often lacked an economic base. In sum, "oligarchical" refers to a style of hegemony that did not necessarily reflect underlying roots of a productive, economic nature.

The power of the oligarchy was based on the use of a varied repertoire of violence and arbitrariness and marked by constant internal clashes. Nineteenth-century Central American history is replete with intra-oligarchical conflicts. Indeed Liberal/Conservative "oligarchical" struggles—particularly those of Honduras and Nicaragua—have continued into the contemporary period. In Nicaragua, however, that feuding ended in July 1979.

In the three decades following the end of World War II, Central American society underwent substantial and relatively rapid change. A modernization process took place, marked by inequalities inherent to agrarian societies in the early throes of "progress." That process was stimulated largely by external economic and political influences and was managed domestically—to its own benefit—by the agrarian bourgeoisie.

As a result of those changes, the settlement of bourgeois accounts with the old oligarchic regime was achieved in neither the Jacobite manner—as might have occurred in Guatemala had President Jacobo Arbenz's expropriations been consolidated—nor the Prussian manner, as the Salvadoran experience seemed to suggest. For in El Salvador, changes were promoted by and for various entrepreneurs belonging to the so-called fourteen families. Actually, the latter case is an optimal illustration of a most important and decisive aspect, a key to understanding of the Central American crisis: the concrete historical significance of changes undergone by the dominant classes over the course of the postwar decades.

Those changes took place during a period of both rural and urban modernization. In the countryside, postwar agricultural diversification was accompanied by the mechanization of agricultural enterprises. Meanwhile in the cities, by the late 1950s, a manufacturing sector was taking shape within the framework of the Central American integration project. That project also enabled various service-sector companies to modernize, increasing both their efficiency and coverage. Banking and financial systems stood out as primary benefactors in that sector. The project was accompanied by a generalized functional diversification of state activities and quantitative growth of the state apparatus. That vast combination of changes gave rise not only to social differentiation but also to an apparent, though slow, modernization of the economic foundations of class domination.

The oligarchic crisis must be placed within this contradictory framework. It was contradictory because, though its economic roots changed, nothing was done to overcome traditional forms of political control. The crisis of the oligarchy, therefore, has evolved over an extended period of time, and should be considered a contradictory stage of transition to a purer bourgeois phase.

The most important internal change occurred with the appearance of financially significant zones of agrarian capitalism. Their growth brought about the modernization of productive forces through the incorporation of new technology and the presence of investment capital in the old coffee plantations. Meanwhile the growth of industrial demand and intraregional trade contributed to a reduction in the importance of land lease as a source of income for the large landowner, who had recognized the opportunity to expand into other productive activities. The new family-based economic groups are the best examples of that synthesis of rent, profit, and interest.

In any case, the gradual and decidedly incomplete transformation of oligarchical into bourgeois groups was never accompanied by modifications of the social relations of production. The presence and active participation of the campesinos in those backward relations continued to be significant, representing a prolongation of the previous period.

The overexploitation of the labor force also continued, using the same old forms of extraction of the surplus product. With the end of easily available land—that is, the takeover of former "zones of refuge" by the expanding cultivation of export crops—the average size of small private plots declined, while underemployment in the countryside increased. The "campesino problem" thereby underwent a qualitative change. Given the limitations of an underdeveloped economy, their numbers and their misery became an issue with no real solution.

It is important to recognize here that the appearance of a vast number of semiproletarianized peasants was not the result of agricultural stagnation. Rather, it was the direct consequence of the nature of capitalist advances in the agrarian sector, as primary-export agriculture consolidated its position because of the continual attractiveness of foreign markets.

Within this process the old bourgeois, commercial coffee grower did not disappear, nor was he destroyed. Instead, the dominant class modified itself slightly. What occurred was an internal restructuring—both slow and painful—that transformed the old landlord-capitalist into a capitalist-landlord.

Costa Rica underwent the most complete bourgeois change in the region because those modifications took place within the context of a mediating, modernizing state. That state was the expression of class alliances in which leading roles were played by the midlevel bourgeoisie, progressive intellectuals, and a campesino sector that had partially benefited from the bourgeois change.

The situation was somewhat different in the rest of Central America, where the oligarchic decomposition evolved in such a way that it might be labeled "agrarian counterrevolution." That is, the campesinos were the ones who paid the heavy price in a modernization process whose top priority was the development of modern methods of repression and control, and whose repercussions included an ossification of the political system. Thus, although there were changes, those changes were marked by the fear of popular revolt.

Other Economic Factors:
The Years of Sustained Growth

Due to the impossibility of tracing a comprehensive picture of Central American economic growth, the objective here will be to highlight some key aspects of that process during the 1960s and 1970s. Those years were exceptional ones in the economic history of the region because—despite ups and downs—a sustained growth was maintained. That growth was due to external factors that only weakened in the wake of generalized international economic disorder in the latter part of the period.

In any case, though the steady pace of economic change was no mean accomplishment, it was achieved at the cost of exacerbating social problems left over from the period of coffee expansion. The slow and incomplete capitalist development of agricultural exports did not act as a "locomotive," pulling the rest of the agricultural sector along behind it. To the contrary, the sector producing basic grains for popular consumption was neglected, leading to declines in production for the domestic market. At the same time, food crop cultivation became increasingly limited to the campesino sectors of the respective national economies.

Furthermore, agricultural production intended for local consumption—such as salary goods and primary industrial materials—maintained low levels of mechanization and was reduced to the worst lands, with access to neither credit nor state assistance. Thus the tendency toward a heightened heterogeneity in the forms of agricultural production was accentuated during those years.

Agricultural capitalism developed in large- and middle-size properties in Central America but has coexisted with, and taken advantage of, the remaining mercantile economy. Indeed today's market has become more deeply linked to that precapitalist sector in order to exploit it better. For a long time the system just described—a modern export economy coexisting with a backward domestic-market agriculture—was able to function without the export sector's transfering its profits to the sector producing goods for domestic consumption. The dynamism of foreign trade provided selective benefits.

The wage levels of the work force as well as the costs of production in general depended—as much in the country as in the city—upon the meager forces of the campesino economy. However, the crisis of the global capitalist market and the consequent low prices for export commodities have demonstrated yet again the vulnerability of the region's economies, their openness to international economic influences, and the profound weaknesses of the primary-export model in particular. Actually, the international crisis did little more than reveal profound internal imbalances that had never been resolved. The brief cycles of expansion, in effect, permitted bourgeois amnesia concerning the campesino problem.

At this point it is worthwhile recalling that the population of Central America doubled during those twenty years, while the "agricultural frontier" finally disappeared. In other words, and contrary to official opinion—national as well as that of international organizations—the economic crisis cannot be explained merely as a result of declining foreign trade.

Independent of that decline, the impoverishment of the campesino population, in both relative and absolute terms (and expressed as an incomplete process of generalized proletarianization), had more or less reached its limits. This meant that land was no longer the fulcrum of any possible solution to the agrarian crisis, nor even the basis of campesino demands. Economic "malformation" had been so severe that social problems had not only accumulated, they had also become insoluble in strictly economic terms.

Consider, for example, that forty of every one hundred families living in the countryside have either lost their land or been left with an amount insufficient for the maintenance of their traditional forms of subsistence. Temporary employment has turned into permanent unemployment for one of every three campesinos over the age of eighteen. The housing deficit never diminished and has recently worsened along with levels of malnutrition, illiteracy, and infant mortality. And all of this has occurred within a social context bereft of civil and political rights.

The problems of the agrarian structural crisis, therefore, cannot be considered merely as economic problems. They originated in the economic order and then became converted into obstacles to growth, blocking social development. An analysis of the agricultural sector limited merely to economic statistics would produce the following results: a rather significant 5.1 percent average annual rate of growth during the 1960s; 3.8 percent between 1971 and 1976; and −3.4 percent per year after 1979.[3]

The previous set of considerations should not be seen as problems that arise from the region's economic "arrears." To view those considerations in such a way—thereby reducing them to the level of a technological problem—might have been appropriate in the past. Today, however, social "backwardness" is an element of the overall political nature of the general crisis racking Central American society.

That backwardness is part of a historical context within which the response to social difficulties has never maintained the necessary tempo, leaving only two equally difficult alternatives: either greater misery, which would mean biological degradation as well as the degeneration of an entire social group; or protest, implying the organization of the malcontents and popular struggle. Here it should be made clear that revolution is never explained by the misery of the masses alone, just as the latter's complaints will never be absent once the insurrection is under way.

It is important to recognize, in relation to the problems created and/or exacerbated by economic growth in recent decades, that the agrarian sector has not been the only generator of dynamism and crisis. At the edges of that sector, a program of industrial development was initiated—relatively successfully—in the early 1960s. In practice, the program of economic integration satisfied regional demand for nondurable consumer goods and a variety of intermediate goods, effectively substituting in part for local artisan production and in part for the previous importation of those goods.

The common market project attained a high level of initial dynamism because of the double mechanism of state protection and physical expansion of the regional market. Today we know, via the troublesome evidence of actual events, that the splendor of manufacturing had been internally sabotaged in advance, provoking a descent into crisis before political effects began to take their toll.

Essentially what happened was that, on the one hand, traditional imports were displaced by other imports—such as intermediate goods required by the new local industries—thereby aggravating the region's chronic commercial deficit. That in turn affected the balance of payments, leading directly to a massive foreign debt. On the other hand, an entrepreneurial model of industrial development emerged that lacked any attention to the needs of balanced, complementary expansion within the region, resulting in an absurd competition at the level of individual nations.

The inevitable outcome was a highly concentrated distribution of profits from intraregional trade, benefiting one or two countries more than others. Though the economic integration of Central America did not produce the strengthening of tendencies toward the concentration of income, neither did it deter them. Nor did it prevent unemployment from becoming a structural element of the urban economy. After 1970, in a slow but nonetheless tragic manner, urban misery took the form of widespread underemployment and unemployment, which led to the growth of an informal sector of the economy.

In the 1970s the agrarian crisis and the weaknesses of the Central American Common Market became more evident because the international crisis accentuated many critical local problems. To begin with, there was a decrease in the dynamism of intraregional trade, a decrease that produced stagnation in the industrial sector. At the same time, a decline in foreign demand for agricultural products meant falling prices for coffee and other export goods. Moreover, as the export sector's decline occurred side by side with an already debilitated basic-grain-producing sector, agrarian production as a whole suffered absolute regression.

Meanwhile, rising prices for gasoline, combined with defensive political maneuvers by the developed countries, struck directly at the heart of the regional economy. Foreign debt mounted continually, accompanied by fiscal and current account deficits (along with diminishing currency reserves) due to the exigencies of repayment mechanisms. Inflation also appeared in the early 1970s, affecting the region's various social classes to differing degrees. And current indicators give no reason to expect improvement in the years to come.

The Political Crisis Begins:
Cracks in the System of Domination

It was suggested earlier in this chapter that the political power of the Central American oligarchy was not always stable. Military dictatorship was yet another form of instability. In the 1930s the resort to military dictators maintained through violent means the threatened social order. It is now well known that the price of that solution was economic stagnation, which lasted until the beginning of the postwar period. In the meantime there was both a partial reactivation of the local campesino economy and a virtual asphyxia of social and cultural life.

With the end of World War II, stirrings toward democracy were accompanied by rising coffee prices. The agrarian classes, boosted by unexpected profits, were able to confront a political offensive that, without doubt, marked the beginning of their crisis. After 1945 in each of the Central American countries—though in different ways—demands began to be made for party organization and political integration. That is, there was a political opening, as it is called these days. Outlets were being sought for both previously existing social forces and those that had been formed only recently, during the preceding period of dictatorial suffocation.

It was a struggle to gain the possibility of real political participation and consequently took the form of either an open or a stifled confrontation with the oligarchy. It was the moment of exemplary leadership—of the "revolutionary half hour"—for a generation of middle-class politicians. It was they who headed the struggles for political democracy, for popular organization, for the establishment of a state based on proper legal foundations and focused on carrying out its socioeconomic functions.

There were also efforts to draw up programs of national culture, to increase access to education, to expand electoral participation of minority groups, and to strengthen municipal and university autonomy. All of these demands were resisted in one way or another, amid conflicts that often lacked clear winners or losers. Taken as a whole, those demands were considered impermissible by the guardians of traditional landlord culture.

That battle within the superstructure inevitably produced new political actors. The participatory presence of new or renovated social forces was most evident in the activity of the urban middle classes. Those classes revealed themselves more clearly through the conflicts they led than through the material conditions of their existence. They were conscious of opportunities presented at the time and took advantage of them to pursue a new version of legality. Their intention was to render old ideological principles—never brought to bear by the late nineteenth-century liberal reformism—less declaratory and formal.

In any case, it certainly was not the campesinos who were at the center of the antioligarchic offensive. To the contrary, the campesinos at that point continued to act—without realizing it—as a "natural" social bastion for their class enemies. But from those first moments on, there was a continual political presence of professionals and university students, of progressive members of the urban artisan sector and the political bureaucracy, as well as that of some midlevel shopkeepers and industrial owners. In addition—and of primary importance—there was the active participation by intellectual groups.

Also taking part in the newly forming organizations were groups composed of industrial and agricultural workers, as well as other semi-proletarianized social sectors from the city, all of which belonged to the so-called popular classes. The common people, in accordance with the attitudes of the time, were always led and represented by leaders from the middle class.

The way in which the oligarchical crisis emerged, from the 1950s on, explains the later course of each country's history. Though a criticism of the entire oligarchic structure was realized only in Guatemala, political-ideological declarations in the face of state power (or of the prevailing style of domination) became more frequent.

There was indeed, then, an antioligarchical offensive, but of a strictly doctrinal character. The coffee economy and its underlying agrarian structure were functioning once again with relative success, which perhaps served to hide—for the time being—those weaknesses inherent to the primary-export model.

As it is unnecessary to give a global account of the region's early postwar history, the following discussion will highlight various political events relative to the oligarchical crisis; for the crisis arose at that moment, with no apparent solution. Here it is important to remember that the popular struggle against the military dictators—supported by the oligarchy—was successful in Guatemala, in El Salvador, and to some extent in Honduras.

The antidictatorial process was most radical in Guatemala, where the discredited army of the Jorge Ubico regime was partially dismantled and replaced, as of 1947, by a more technical and professional institution. From that point on, the army received U.S. aid and inspiration. The Liberal party also disappeared, and the political game was opened to free popular organization. The agrarian reform of 1952, and the expropriations of uncultivated United Fruit Company lands in 1953, marked the culminating moments of the democratic, antioligarchic and anti-imperialist movement.

Although the downfall of that popular movement, in 1954, did not constitute a restoration of the system headed by General Ubico, it did re-establish the overwhelming power and influence of the coffee growers and of the most backward agrarian sectors of Guatemalan society in general.

In El Salvador, the downfall of General Maximiliano Hernández Martínez—who had been responsible for the slaughter of 30,000 campesinos in 1932—also occurred at the hands of a multiclass coalition of national dimension, headed by professionals and young military officers. However, by April and May 1944, the strength of the popular movement had been reduced by the discovery and execution of the movement's leaders by the dictatorship.[4]

The crisis manifested itself primarily within the army itself, rather than in the streets, and was decided in favor of the most reactionary groups. It was not until the "Colonel's Coup" of 1948, led by Colonel Oscar Osorio—and without the annoyance of mobilized masses—that steps were finally taken to democratize Salvadoran political life at the level of the state and to promote significant economic growth. Here a modernizing military accepted the task of halting the antioligarchic offensive in its initial tracks, eventually carrying out gradual, but decidedly insufficient, reforms.

The antioligarchic struggles in Honduras were of a lesser dimension, limited to combat against the military dictatorship of General Tiburcio Carías. In the political sphere at that moment, the strength of neither the landowners nor the military was pervasive. An alliance of the state and foreign banana plantations provided sufficiently stable foundations for a traditional caudillo regime that could not be overthrown by the type of popular coalitions that triumphed in Guatemala and El Salvador.

It was not until 1964, with the civil and constitutional government of Ramón Villeda Morales, that the country enjoyed its first democratic experiences; and not until 1972, under General Oswaldo López Arellano, were some modifications of the agrarian structure attempted. This situation helps to explain, in part, why acute forms of political crisis— which appeared in the three bordering countries—did not surface in Honduras in the mid-1970s.

The Nicaraguan experience was particularly important. A significant train of events began in 1943—at the turning point of World War II— when Somoza had himself reelected for the first time. One year later the first protest movement appeared, led by the Conservative Youth. The Nicaraguan oligarchy, however, managed to definitively skirt those troubles via the "Somoza solution," imposed by North American intervention.

Though a "conservative" faction of the Conservative party remained in constant opposition to Anastasio Somoza García, successive offshoots of that same party served as his electoral accomplices as often as was necessary. And despite the party's opposition, the overall antioligarchic thrust of Conservative efforts was scarce or nonexistent. The party was indeed anti-*Somoza*, but progressive reforms—a democratic order, the end of landed estates, the sociopolitical integration of the nation—were not on their agenda. They attempted to solve Nicaragua's portion of the regional political crisis within the state itself, under the aegis of "Somoza I" (Anastasio Somoza García). Due largely to their influence—and despite the dictator's personal control—Somoza was unable to have himself reelected in 1947,[5] though he did retain command of the National Guard. After a brief interim period, however, he took direct control of the government once again.

The other decisive element for an understanding of why the political crisis was postponed is of an economic nature: the cotton boom, which began in the mid-1940s. It was a period of growth in production and exports unparalleled in the economic history of the region. With the creation of that primary-export sector—which benefited both elite factions—intraoligarchic differences became secondary. In effect, economic growth postponed the political crisis.

Finally, there was the Costa Rican experience, which differed from others in the region because the economic activities of its oligarchic groups were more closely tied to commercial capital (that is, control of coffee processing and exports) than to extensive landownership. The existence of a considerable proportion of middle- and small-size coffee producers added a participative, democratic dimension to political life. Social control was not achieved by force, but rather through education, religion, and the ideology of campesino equality.

The 1948 civil war provided the opportunity for a subsequent accommodation between leaders of democratic political processes and those forces whose priority was an economic modernization of the oligarchy. In effect, the oligarchic crisis never really occurred because of the society's democratic tradition and because during the 1950s the coffee growers' economic role was redefined. Costa Rica therefore constituted a notable exception, demonstrating that even a rural society permeated by conservative values can undertake political modernization without having to endure fractures of any greater severity than the brief civil war of 1948.

Between the end of World War II and the beginning of the crisis in the 1970s each society in the region—particularly the Guatemalan, the Salvadoran, and the Nicaraguan—underwent intense periods of popular agitation. That agitation indicated a gradual erosion in the system of domination and led to the imposition of a "state of emergency" in the precise sense of the term: a state response to deepening social crisis.

In effect, a variety of "grains" sown in the past were reaped in the 1970s. Those grains included collective aspirations failed, violence, and death—each of which fed a harvest of anticipated conflict. And thus the lesson of early democratic challenges was that the fruits of political activity were no better than those of the economic sphere. As a result, many people came to the conclusion that it was worse to die of hunger, via submission, than to die of a bullet wound, via defiance. The preceding phrase sounds like a line taken from a war novel. It corresponds, however, to a state of mind that emerged initially in the combativeness of isolated groups from the petit bourgeois urban sector. Their opposition in turn became collective impatience during the 1970s. That conversion from isolated combativeness to collective impatience will be the focus of the following section's analysis.

The social forces that had raised antioligarchical banners back in the 1950s, seeking to consolidate or amplify democratic political participation, were crushed again and again. That experience differs from the political democracy that has been able to function in some other Latin American countries.

In those countries a competitive system of state governance has been able to survive due to the presence of adequate forms of lower-class mobilization and participation, regardless of the control mechanisms that may have been employed. The repertoire of those organizational forms has varied but has always included an electoral process capable of absorbing tensions and producing a collective sensation of participation. The populist experiences in the Southern Cone, in particular, provide examples of control and channeling of social conflicts. Meanwhile those of Venezuela and Mexico have offered examples—not always subtle— of the co-optation of the working class and other groups.

In Latin America as a whole, all known democratic experiences have been marked by two kinds of phenomena. On the one hand, they have partially satisfied some of the demands of various social groups; on the other, they have regulated electoral participation to include a tolerated opposition.

In Central America, however—with the exception of Costa Rica— this has not occurred. The region's movements for democracy have been definitively blocked from top to bottom, under a system of domination that constantly oversees the exclusion of new forces in order to maintain the hegemonic position of the dominant class. That exclusion is achieved via recourse to violent means that frequently represent direct negations of the system's own formal legalities.

It can be said, in summary, that the frustrated efforts of the immediate postwar period—the initial struggles for democracy and reform—were resumed during the 1970s. Pluralism under the control of bourgeois culture, in effect, proved to be as shortsighted as was company management toward trade union organization and demands. Within that limited bourgeois perspective, the possibility of allowing for the spread of a "social-democratic style" became both dangerous and unnecessary. That bourgeois intransigence prevented the creation of mechanisms capable of mediating interclass and class/state differences. As a consequence of that void, demands for higher wages became political issues of national scope, eventually taking the form of a challenge to the entire established order.

Lacking the political culture that only sustained democratic practice can create, the Central American nations with their system of domination in general—and the state's administration of society in particular—continued to exhibit an oligarchic character, resorting to repressive and antirepresentative responses. Because of that pattern, antioligarchic struggles appeared to become entangled with economic demands of a more bourgeois nature, eventually uniting to form a single crisis.

The tendency toward a political polarization of social struggles has allowed the most backward sectors of the agrarian elite to dictate the ideological defense of the existing order. Thus the policies emerging from the heart of the dominant groups have continued to support the futile defense of a system based upon the unproductive monopoly of the land and the gratuitous exploitation of the campesino.

In Guatemala and El Salvador today, the remnants of the oligarchy—the most socially backward landowner groups—continue producing ideology. It is they who furiously defend the political order, with the pretext of saving private property, nothing more. By defending private property, they seek to protect not only their right to territorial monopoly and their right to lease land as they see fit, but also their right to be obeyed. It is that determination—further aggravated by the violence of class conflict—that constitutes the very core of the crisis; it is that determination that has been defied. Thus within the whirlwind of the Central American crisis—which exploded in Nicaragua, El Salvador, and Guatemala in the mid-1970s—it was the most conservative groups of landowners that determined the battle plans for the survival of all.

However, those plans were hardly the product of bourgeois unity, or an example of lucidity in the face of "the tempest unleashed." On this point it has been suggested that the survival instinct momentarily induced the bourgeois factions to act together. In any case, the internal belligerence around which the dominant class rallied was a decisive element of the crisis.

As a consequence, the struggle of the 1970s represented a synthesis of various processes. The failures of the postwar "impossible democratization" process, for example, combined with the later defeats and repression suffered by popular movements each time they attempted to organize themselves toward political or economic ends.

The experiences of the first wave of guerrilla groups were also a part of that synthesis. Guevarist military strategies known as *foquismo* (guerrilla strategy of igniting revolution through small groups—*focos*—leading struggles in the countryside) clearly brought valuable lessons, though primarily for what these strategies failed to do rather than for what they did.

Finally—as already discussed—there was the intersection of effects originating in the two aspects of the economic crisis. One aspect was internal and structural, the product of the national history of each country. The other was external, the product of a negative international juncture that impacted equally on the entire region.

Reflections on the Revolutionary Popular Movement

The diverse processes alluded to above became unified upon the concrete terrain of social struggles and the revolutionary movement. As the magnitude of the popular protest grew, the protest also gained autonomy, revealing an extraordinary organic and political imagination. Here it is worthwhile recalling the observation that the objective determining factors manifested by a structural crisis can only be expressed politically if they coincide with subjective determining factors such as organization, leadership, and programs of mobilization. Political activity retains its autonomy, and only through those subjective channels can a structural crisis becomes an open crisis.

The following will be an examination of the most outstanding characteristics of the popular movement: of its program, of its ideology, and especially, of its component sectors. The first point to consider is the role that workers and campesinos have played in contemporary processes feeding the crisis. And here it should be remembered that Central American societies are marked by the presence of a backward, campesino majority and a small, unskilled proletariat. The question, then, is whether class consciousness develops among a proletariat whose existence is irrelevant to the way capitalism functions within society and whose organization is weak or nonexistent. In Central America the working class and its most advanced sectors have gradually adopted revolutionary positions *before* their class consciousness was fully developed.

Revolutionary conduct emerged as the result of the diverse ways in which social struggle had been organized in earlier years, years in which class-oriented demands, in the strict sense of the term, had not necessarily appeared. Of course, the development of political consciousness does not correspond to the structural conditions of a given class, but rather to its concrete historical experiences, that is, to the nature of the political processes of which that class has become a part.

Thus the mobilization of Central American workers did not occur because of their superior levels of class consciousness, but because they were moved by the strength and ideology of a revolutionary popular process. The same thing has occurred with other social forces that have become involved in the region's present revolutionary process. The entirety of those social groupings—among them, workers, campesinos, students, and intellectuals—will be called "revolutionary popular movements" in order to distinguish them from national liberation movements, populism, and popular national movements of other societies.

How do revolutionary popular movements differ from other multiclass opposition movements? In Central America, other than a few fleeting exceptions, there have been no populist experiences. This has been due to the absence of a bourgeois faction capable of successfully sponsoring popular demands—the aim being to manipulate dominated sectors either politically or electorally—in order to strengthen its position within the interbourgeois struggle. The bourgeoisie was only able to control the working class and the popular masses through violence. Given the circumstances, the bourgeoisie was either unable or saw no need to turn to populist management.

In any case, the populist phenomenon is an essentially urban experience that does not occur in predominantly agrarian societies. It has been a political phenomenon typical of societies that rapidly initiated their industrialization process at the moment of oligarchic retreat. In those societies, popular participation has taken the form of populism when their urban masses first became politically active. Once mobilized, the masses were then "maneuvered," much like decisive battalions, within a strategy intended to guarantee the political representation of other interests.

Revolutionary popular movements have evolved in times of crisis. That crisis, by its very nature, can develop only in societies where the most backward sectors of the landowner faction are in close alliance with other bourgeois factions and are unable to control the working class through normal mechanisms of liberal democracy. Furthermore, revolutionary popular movements are the expression of a delayed oligarchic crisis accompanied by a premature bourgeois crisis. They develop where the working class—limited in number—lacks any organic tradition, and where the majority of the population is composed of campesinos. Finally, in these societies a significant faction of the midlevel sectors—marginalized by the authoritarian tradition—can become indisputable leaders by merging with the other dominated sectors, with groups often referred to as the "common people" (*pueblo*).

The revolutionary popular mobilization as it has evolved in Central America is not the result of extreme class antagonism, nor does its energy spring merely from the "classic" contradiction between capital and labor. The strength of the workers' movement is evident, but that strength has developed within a framework of political antagonism—a substitute for underlying economic antagonism—that served to avoid direct confrontation with the "exploiting bourgeoisie." Social conflicts were produced at different locations within the economic structure but were resolved on the political terrain, where the role of the state took precedence over class.

In effect, the working class has shared social, political, and cultural experiences with other more numerous social sectors. The proletariat represents only a minority faction within a larger working-class majority. That majority, in turn—exploited by capital in various ways—also includes sectors that have not undergone those same experiences, but that have nonetheless shared basic contradictions within the system of domination. For all working-class sectors have been defined less by conditions of exploitation than by those of domination. Their unity has been built around protest activities mounted together as well as a multiclass, revolutionary popular ideology.

Historically, "class consciousness" has meant *potential* class consciousness. In other words, there has always existed the possibility that a subordinate class would acquire the determination to act in a way that directly and clearly affected the opposing interests of the dominant class(es), with the subordinate class thereby being transformed into the active social agent of a political program.

In Central America, the specific working-class response to that class antagonism eventually took the form of concrete actions. And those actions proved to be capable of developing a class consciousness that initially had been nothing more than a possibility. The campesinos and the working class in general, but especially the middle sectors—including intellectuals—developed their potential consciousness during the crisis. However, this was not necessarily the kind of class consciousness that theory would lead one to expect; that is, worker consciousness.[6]

The originality and richness of the revolutionary movements of the 1970s can only be understood by recalling, once again, what has been an essential element of the crisis: the conjunction of old antioligarchic demands with the offensive against the bourgeois order. The latter characteristic, of course, was expressed more via methods of struggle than through familiar political programs.

By attacking the oligarchy, popular forces have confronted the bourgeoisie and eventually taken on the state itself. Meanwhile, the methods employed—armed struggle—correspond to the most acute form of class struggle, meaning the effective revision and regeneration of the political-ideological program in accordance with the course of those historic actions.

This process in turn explains why the revolutionary movements, exploding onto the scene in the 1970s, displaced their initial battlefronts and became converted—by force of concrete events and conditions as well as by previous experiences—into national and revolutionary movements. Those movements were marked by an anticapitalist stance that arose less from doctrine than from their rejection of the existing system in toto, a system that had a particularly forceful impact on the experiences of the masses.

What were those specific experiences that, when combined, produced a redefinition of both the form and content of social contradictions? There exists a wide diversity of experiences—most of which were frustrated—within the history of the workers' movement. For years it was the bearer of economic demands through local organizations and trade unions. But those initiatives ended in defeat, without the slightest concession. Failure brought home the harsh reality of capital-labor antagonism, which had become ever more evident in the struggle for the appropriation of surplus value.

The Central American working class, as previously pointed out, has been small in number and short on organic experiences. In contrast, however, its considerable past as an exploited class has been significant, replete with struggle, demands made of large landowners (*la patronal*) and resistance to police repression. It is also worthwhile to recall an unusual characteristic that trade union conflicts have assumed in the region: that is, their tendency to go beyond the limits of what could be considered strictly class contradictions, quickly attaining a general, universal level of political struggle for democracy and freedom.

In any case, failed union demands for higher salaries and better working conditions were not the popular movements' only frustrating experiences. Equally important were those that occurred in the struggle for electoral participation. Here it is necessary to recall the sectarian nature of the "pluralism" of anticommunist democracy as well as the obstacles facing the establishment of a reformist alternative, stemming from the lack of political space. In sum, the failures of political struggles—due to an intolerance of any pacific, predictable form of opposition—served to expand discontent and antagonism.

Finally, there are the experiences of the Central American campesino, who was "formed" as the direct product—in the form of a servile work force—of the oligarchic period and "deformed" during the period of capitalist modernization, as a semiproletariat. In both situations, the campesino was something less than a citizen.

Having taken account of both urban and rural working-class sectors, then, it would seem that all paths converged on a propitious point for active opposition to the system. Actual experiences have been as diverse as the different class factions that compose the popular movements. All have met with immediate opposition from the state's forces of order. And here the underlying weakness of the region's bourgeois state reveals itself: The dominant class defines itself both within and through the state. Sooner rather than later, the dominated classes must therefore confront the state, thereby defying the system as a whole.

Popular revolutionary ideology has been a mobilizing multiclass force precisely because it has gathered up the entire gamut of complaints and demands of defeated as well as semivictorious struggles, giving them a national political character that is at once radical and universal. State repression and violence inevitably reinforced the revolutionary nature of the popular reaction. And it is from that context of violence and political frustration that the primary ideological characteristic of the revolutionary popular movement emerged: its profoundly antiauthoritarian and prodemocratic character.

Struggles for democracy and freedom, therefore—for an end to despotism, arbitrariness, and the lack of fundamental security guarantees— are political goals that have attracted multiclass support. Those goals, as well as the kinds of struggles they imply, cannot be explained merely as an unusual explosion of class hatred. Rather, they must be seen as an inevitable outgrowth of the will to rebel, as a collective desire expressed in the form of a popular movement whose point of reference is political power and whose ultimate objective is popular power (*poder popular*), that is, a government of the common people.

The contradiction between democracy and dictatorship certainly does not represent a class contradiction. However, the contradiction between ruling types has become the locus of ideological mobilization because it is more inclusive than the bourgeois/proletarian antagonism. At the same time, existing social polarization in Central American society has converted the contradiction between the common people and the dominant classes into the "final antagonism," the decisive element of the current crisis. Though particular characteristics of economic growth were related to the consolidation of this type of contradiction, most important of all was the way in which the hegemony of the dominant class became established. Here it should be repeated that a class ideology is only born from existing social conditions, from class actions, and from class struggles. As a consequence, antidictatorial, antioligarchic struggle has been transformed into a prodemocratic ideology. And due to the character that class confrontation has assumed, the demands have become radical, with the democratic struggle coming to mean the struggle for popular power, for a new kind of democracy—alluded to above—oriented toward the need of the poor majority.

The programs of the political-military organizations leave no doubt about those objectives, though the particular experiences of the various national struggles produce differences from one regional confrontation to another. An example of those differences can be seen in the case of

Nicaragua, where power was in the hands of Somoza's personalized dictatorship. The breadth of the anti-Somoza social coalition was unparalleled in the history of Central America.

As a result, the contradiction between the common people and the dominant class—which was a determining factor in Nicaragua's struggle—has acquired a different sense in El Salvador and Guatemala, because the dividing line separating those social groups has been less inclusive and less visible in the latter countries. It would be worthwhile explaining those differences in another way. In Guatemala and El Salvador, the bourgeoisie (including its diverse factions) has managed to create "facade democracies." That is, there have been governments chosen via formal electoral processes in which the game between political parties was not only reduced to the level of right-wing anticommunist tirades but also included outright fraud, interspersed with interclass violence and the occasional coup d'état. These political charades have been bereft of true popular participation.

However, it would be foolish not to recognize that anticommunism and the management of a symbolism tied to negative aspects of Soviet society have succeeded in limiting some social sectors' breadth of vision. This explains why an astute right wing is able to campaign with a certain level of popular support.

Another problem—which is not only theoretical but also strategic—is to figure out what is meant by the term "common people" within the framework of a revolutionary popular mobilization such as that which has taken place in Central America. For there was a stage within that lengthy process—culminating in the mid-1970s—in which mobilization and protest abandoned their former spontaneous, isolated character and began to take on a more homogeneous, collective, and independent behavior. All those mobilized through that process, then, are the "common people." As social actors they represent a multiplicity of social interests that—though different—are not contradictory. A broader convergence of popular objectives is as relevant within this process as is the ever-greater specificity of class interests.

Here it is useful to recall the use of the term "common people" in its Maoist sense, understood as referring to those national classes that have been exploited and dominated by the system. Those classes constitute an aggregate of social forces whose strength lies precisely in their heterogeneity. That is because by acting together they become defined by a common enemy, in turn defining themselves within a unity of political mobilization and popular revolutionary ideology.

The contradiction between the people and the dominant classes differs from that which is expressed in populism, because in popular revolutionary ideology the interests of the dominated class determine the fundamental objectives of the opposition to the system and are pursued to their ultimate consequences. In populist ideology, in contrast, the interests of an advanced bourgeois faction end up dictating the final course of political action.

The revolutionary popular movements have clearly demonstrated an unusual, particular form of class struggle, which they neither deny nor conceal. Their opposition has been formed in broader contradictory terms vis-à-vis the bourgeoisie, and they have sought to attain a national scope via the generalization of conflicts.

As previously mentioned, together with the prodemocratic character of popular revolutionary ideology we also find the anti-imperialist aspect, an essential element of its ideological discourse. The strength of that anti-imperialism varies, depending on the depth of its historical roots, with the radical example being that of Sandinism. In general, however, the anti-imperialist characteristic is present in the form of a primary, fundamental component of national identity.

The anti-imperialist ideology of the revolutionary popular movement should not be confused—at least at the level of theoretical analysis— with the contradictions and forms of that ideology adopted by national liberation movements. In the latter, the relationship between colonies and colonized—or between metropole and dominated nation—permeates everything, redefining class alliances as well as the course of political action taken by those alliances. National liberation movements are generally headed by a non-*comprador* faction of the local bourgeoisie (those who are interested not only in personal enrichment but also in advancing democracy, justice, and social progress), due to the historical existence of a national bourgeoisie.

The anti-imperialist content of the revolutionary popular movements' ideology, however, has been derived from specific historical experiences in which capital and North American policy founded enduring alliances with the oligarchy. For example, the alliance maintained by foreign capital via control of the banana plantation—the so-called foreign enclave—cut the state's sovereign jurisdiction. Concessions to the enclave also pared any sense of national integration. The first social struggles involving agricultural workers in Central America arose in the face of foreign capital, and the first class consciousness among dominated social sectors grew out of struggles against foreign domination.

Today, those bourgeois-international alliances go well beyond the economic realm, where foreign capital is, in any case, the owner of the most advanced sector of national industry. There are also political and strategic dimensions, expressed through multiform support to the dominant class (to its army, the public sector, and so on). Therefore, in the contradiction between the common people and the dominant class, imperialist interests clearly lie on one side of the dividing line. One need only consider, for example, the present condition of the Salvadoran state, which has been converted into a protectorate.

Anti-imperialism in Central America also derives from the region's geopolitical condition: from its proximity to the United States and from its shores on the Caribbean Sea. That geopolitical condition has bestowed the isthmus with a strategic importance that goes beyond any economic or cultural considerations.

Resisting Manifest Destiny, then, has served to imbue popular anti-imperialism with a sense of both ideological and active recuperation of the national program. This is not mere sentimentalism but rather a firm attachment to historical experience. The nationalism of the revolutionary popular movement—in the hands of a broad multiclass alliance by the early 1980s—has thus been part of an antioligarchic, antibourgeois position. And that movement has never abandoned its demands for genuine democracy.

In the Nicaraguan case, all of these elements appear to have been exacerbated. Not only the antidictatorial but also the anti-imperialist struggle took on forms very similar to those of a national liberation movement, due to the pronounced foreign character of the resources—military, economic, political, and cultural—used to maintain class domination.

The presence of the United States in Nicaragua has been multifaceted and ubiquitous. The Marine infantry was stationed there from August 4, 1911, to January 1, 1933, with only a brief interruption.[7] Those circumstances, apart from significantly altering political relations between oligarchic factions, also led to the construction of a system of authority closely tied to external forces. Somoza I was the direct continuation of that intervention. The National Guard—an "American-led constabulary"[8]—as well as Somoza's chief civil and military technocrats were trained in the United States, developing an attachment to that country unknown in the rest of Central America. They tended to consider North America a second homeland, a sort of life insurance policy. In addition, the enterprises of the Somoza Group and other existing joint ventures made foreign capital predominant. Because of all these ties, the strong impression emerges that Nicaragua's national revolutionary mobilization was basically a struggle against a foreign power.

Meanwhile, the processes feeding the crises in El Salvador and Guatemala have been marked by a different chain of contradictions. Those differences are primarily due to the lack of experiences similar to those of Nicaragua and to the higher levels of capitalist development in El Salvador and Guatemala. That development was the result of both an entire century of export-led growth and the fact that those two countries were able to take better advantage of the common market's industrial opportunities.

Anti-imperialism has been present, therefore, but not for the same reasons it arose in Nicaragua. In El Salvador and Guatemala it has not only filled a pragmatic need but has also served as a primary point of political reference. Their anti-imperialism has been an essential element of popular mobilization against class dictatorship, against a system of domination ever more dependent on foreign support. El Salvador in particular has become a de facto foreign protectorate, and diverse forms of direct intervention by the United States only exacerbate national aspects of each conflict, as well as of the crisis in general.

It is necessary to complete this brief presentation by alluding to a characteristic that, in the final analysis, has effectively stimulated the revolutionary popular movements of Central America. Proceeding with caution, our main interest is to determine the particular meaning of the "socialist proclamation" adopted by social protest movements whose most clear and organic expression has been the so-called political-military organization.

Social protest becomes popular insurrection in the form of a revolutionary popular war. But here two clarifications are necessary: First of all, we used the word "proclamation" because it would be quite inappropriate to refer to a socialist *program;* secondly, we introduced the equivocal term "final analysis" because the most intimate nature of these social movements only achieves its final definition through a determining act of negation. That act constitutes a political gesture of rejection in the heart of a sociopolitical order openly fought, disrupted, and discredited by those movements.

It is well known that socialism arose from the beginning as a project based on specific intentions, as a political program whose sustenance was class desire and whose consciousness rested in Marxist thought. Socialism came to mean the passage from utopian visions to the rational explanation introduced by Karl Marx and Friedrich Engels.

In that classical version, it appeared that only the full development of productive forces—that is, a mature capitalism—could give way to the structural necessity of socialism. The proletarian revolution and the proletariat would be the vehicle and the class, respectively, capable of converting that historic potential into action.

In Central America—and in backward regions of the capitalist periphery in general—the course of that political possibility has been different. There, capitalism's limitations have not been defined through its full development, but rather through its stagnation. Dependent capitalism, as it evolved, gradually created a structural situation of permanent and generalized social backwardness, affecting the progressive movement of society.

Central America provides harsh testimony against the global capitalist system to the effect that part of it does not function well, that future generations of the underdeveloped world have no grounds for the modest optimism that would allow them to imagine different social conditions in the future. And it is precisely that kind of thinking that gives substance to the expression "the weakest link in the chain."

One reason for the absence of a significant socialist tradition in Central America is that, for a long time, neither a workers' culture nor political parties had been formed. There socialism remained an intellectual protest, clearly inspired by a doctrinaire Marxism that appeared in association with the Communist parties. The latter were persecuted groups of self-sacrificing artisans, teachers, and university students who—from the underground or from their prison cells—proclaimed socialism as the ideal horizon of the economic process.

The crisis of the 1970s and the emerging revolutionary organizations shared the credit for hastening the advance along the road to utopia. They sought to convert the distant horizon of socialism into an immediate—though diffuse—goal, to give shape to the incomplete image of a better society.

The lack of a socialist (or social-anarchist) tradition should not be understood as a fatal limitation, for it only testifies to a prolonged stage of antioligarchic conflict. That is to say, the historic magnitude of the region's backwardness is revealed by the length and bitterness of the struggle, a struggle against privileges derived from monopoly over the land and in favor of redistributing the surplus produced by the vast campesino masses.

Here it is important to remember the distinction between a movement's objectives and its historical subjects, to consider the specific way in which these elements combine to form national liberation movements. Indeed, those movements appear to be a historical substitute for the classical revolutionary processes of a proletarian character, a natural product of dependent capitalist societies.

Independent of the fact that we have yet to see the "collapse" of an advanced democracy at the hands of the proletariat, there is no doubt that, since the beginning of the postwar era, significant social crises have occurred elsewhere. Important, national-bourgeois/anticolonial movements have arisen from those crises.

In the meantime, differences between those movements and populism—including its most advanced forms—have been established. For unlike national liberation movements, populist social movements—as well as their ideology—sought to modernize the state, to increase its control over the economy, and to apply distribution policies in order to legitimize postoligarchic order.

But the nature of revolutionary popular movements is different again from the other two. Sooner or later, the former create a situation known as "revolutionary popular war," which is the popular response to a social crisis. Their revolutionary character is determined primarily by the predominantly military nature of the political confrontation.

Revolutionary popular war is not a war of liberation because the power that the revolutionaries attempt to destroy is not a foreign colonial power, regardless of the strength of its ties to the U.S. military. Though it shares other movements' multiclass composition, the Central American phenomenon distances itself from them by its radical anticapitalist philosophy.

It should also be stressed that although the "common people" of national liberation struggles are not like classical revolutionary subjects, neither are they like the revolutionary popular subjects. Here leadership and political programs prove to be essential points of divergence. In the first case, the goal is to break off the colonial relationship in order to open new pathways to capitalist development, for which bourgeois leadership is a decisive condition. In the Central American case, however, popular movements are attempting to overcome capitalist underdevelopment, which requires both an end to the bourgeois/imperialist relationship and a leadership motivated by a proletarian ideological hegemony.

Finally, within this wealth of situations and cultural/ideological characteristics, an additional aspect of the Guatemalan popular revolution deserves special mention: the indigenous presence. For national-ethnic demands have been added to the program of struggle and to the most profound sense of the crisis. However, national-ethnic issues are expressed in another way and contain another kind of contradiction. Though class contradictions (campesino/landlord, common people/state) clearly underlie indigenous rebellion, class alone cannot satisfactorily explain the antagonism represented by cultural values and forms of group identification (such as language or dress). And in Guatemala the strength of those factors—as well that antagonism—varies from one ethnic group to another.

Advocating the liberation of the indigenous peoples from cultural domination and racial discrimination has been tantamount to shattering an important ideological component of Guatemalan oligarchic culture. Racism has long helped landowners to dominate society. Incorporating the Indians into the popular movement has meant making them part of the common people, part of the essential contradiction vis-à-vis the dominant class. Stressing the importance of cultural-ethnic values has enriched revolutionary popular ideology and thereby strengthened the popular struggle.

Notes

1. Or in less complex terms, it might be described as the economic way of life that is built atop what Fernand Braudel called "material civilization."

2. This subject has been developed in less precipitous fashion in Chapter 2.

3. See IDB, *El Progreso Económico y Social en América Latina; Informe anual 1980–81* (Inter-American Development Bank, Washington, D.C., 1982), information compiled from various tables.

4. In January 1944 Hernández Martínez had eight young military officers and a group of civilian leaders shot by a firing squad. The general strike of April and May 1944 forced him to resign, whereupon power passed into the hands of another general (Andrés Ignacio Menéndez), who was in turn expelled from the government by a colonel from the most reactionary faction of the army (Osmín Aguirre).

5. Somoza, forced by both domestic and international (U.S.) pressure, approved the candidacy of Leonardo Argüello, who won the elections of February 1947. Two months later Somoza forced him aside and named Benjamín Lacayo Sacasa as his replacement. Twenty-two days later Lacayo Sacasa called for new elections, which were won by Víctor Román y Reyes. Both Lacayo Sacasa and Román y Reyes were uncles of Somoza.

6. Revolutionary popular movements, unique to backward capitalist societies, present many theoretical difficulties if one tries to characterize them only in terms of their class content. Neither their forms of organization, nor the origins of their leadership, nor their programs permit the kind of simplistic analysis in which everything fits within the theoretical limits of a class-based definition.

7. North American entrepreneurs organized the first National Bank of Nicaragua, with headquarters in the state of Delaware. Customs came under the control of the High Commission, in order to assure the repayment of a public debt forced upon Nicaragua shortly after the intervention. The U.S. government also took charge of an important share of state functions: local communications (in an initial period); police and border security; currency and banking, etc.

8. Richard Millet, *Los Guardianes de la Dinastía: historia de la Guardia Nacional de Nicaragua (1925–1965)* (EDUCA, Costa Rica, 1977).

4

Eight Keys to Understanding the Central American Crisis

The Historical Rupture

The profound political crisis of Central America[1] has been shaped by the nature of its social struggles. Those struggles have been the outcome of long-standing processes of economic growth that created structural imbalances, as well as other problems, without ever resolving them. But above all, the crisis has been born of permanently postponed redress of grievances and of repeated violations of human rights. In sum, the crisis spread in the wake of social and political struggles— struggles carried out peacefully and legally, only to be outlawed and repressed by the state.

The situation became particularly acute in the 1970s, when the "accumulation of problems" took on new forms. It was a period characterized by the Central American bourgeoisie's refusal time and again to seek national consensus. Instead that bourgeoisie opted definitively for a type of military dictatorship that maintained a superficial legality in the name of democracy while carrying out extreme forms of state terrorism.

The notion of crisis as an accumulation of problems is only half true because it only partially explains the situation. For a long time the region's dominant class has demonstrated a structural incapacity to adequately resolve the social and political consequences of economic growth. That is, those in power have failed to find a solution to the problems generated by a development path imposed by their own local bourgeois interests as well as those of large-scale international capital. But why, then, did the crisis arise in this region and in the 1980s—and not before—given that long-standing incapacity?

The crisis emerged and developed at the political level and was characterized by an autonomous irruption of the masses into the political arena. This popular presence has been accompanied by extremely violent methods of struggle. Indeed, it has been through armed confrontation that the masses are at last earning a role as subjects of their own history. This is clearly the culmination of a process that effectively prohibits a return to the degree of disorganization that marked previous political forms of domination and control.

Today, then, "equilibrium" cannot be reestablished in the traditional manner: by repressing the masses. The rapid reconstitution of a new type of power in Nicaragua following the downfall of Somoza represented an exemplary case. In El Salvador, the bloody Christian-Democratic experience only proves that room for moderation there has also disappeared. The nature of the accumulated problems themselves—more than the impatience of the masses—has precluded any intermediate solution.

In Guatemala, however, another strategy has been put to the test, though the results increasingly resemble El Salvador's: a complete lack of both reformist initiatives and disposition toward dialogue. In Guatemala the business of politics has been conducted by the dominant class as a zero-sum game in which the smallest concession is considered a defeat.

The political crisis arose as a challenge to continuity, which explains the use of the term "rupture." The *necessary* cause—if the complexity of the phenomenon can be posed in such a way—was the heavy burden of objective factors. Those factors, having been determined by the structures of society itself, eventually became manifest in the consciousness of the dominated masses.

The *sufficient* cause, in turn, was the irruption of the subordinate classes. All possibilities of containing that irruption—including state terrorism—were negated by the political strategies of the popular opposition. The weight of subjective factors—also accumulated through long years of defeat and sacrifice—transformed objective factors into a determination for change. Continuity was no longer possible because the period of "normality" had been exhausted. The crisis surfaced in the form of a collective impatience before evolving into massive displays of civil disobedience by the dominated classes.

Generalized disobedience perhaps best characterizes the process that began to crystallize in the mid-1970s. But from another perspective, the process signified a loss of authority. And authority that is not respected implies a weakening and discrediting of power, a loss of efficiency. Consequently, the state resorted to physical force and the utilization of extreme violence. Central America has offered so many examples of violent repression that illustration is no longer necessary.

Of course, a crisis situation does not necessarily generate a revolutionary situation. However extreme the signs of bourgeois weakness may be in terms of hegemonic capacity, only the well-coordinated strength of the dominated classes can subvert an established order. That is, significant levels of disorder will be provoked only by an organized opposition that has lost confidence in the system.

In effect, the contemporary political crisis is an overwhelming challenge because it takes place precisely in the sphere where the dominant class has constructed and carried out its management of society. But this ensures neither a revolutionary situation nor, much less, the inevitability of victory.

The region's military traditions have disguised a new feature of the critical road undertaken by Central America. Today military dictatorship—the army's control of society—constitutes the institutional embodiment of the crisis, its worst symptom. The focus here is not on the absence of democracy, which always accompanies military rule. Rather, the emphasis falls on the depth and breadth of repression in Central America in recent years.

For the nature of the military phenomenon has changed. In Guatemala, where no war has yet been declared, official repression under the Fernando Romeo Lucas García government alone was responsible for over five thousand political assassinations between 1979 and 1982, including the destruction of peasant villages in the departments of Chimaltenango, Quiché, and Baja Verapaz. In El Salvador, open confrontations between guerrillas and the army were responsible for only 10 percent of the twenty thousand officially registered deaths in the same period. The rest were victims of direct government repression.

Under conditions such as those it has no longer been possible to convert internal antagonism into acceptable forms of participation in order to transform the social conflict into a positive dynamic factor. That antagonism—as a consequence of the official response—has been transformed into total subversion, and its expression has become a force of rupture. These factors have signaled the end of reformist conceptions and a break with all previously existing forms of political organization of the subordinate classes.

A new combination of forms of struggle has emerged, therefore, along with the discovery of new arenas for political action and a maturity capable of establishing the conditions for united efforts at least over the medium term. What this has come to mean is action in the present with a vision of the future, the goal being to convert a historic breaking point into an opportunity for real departure.

The Years of Defeat and Despair

At the beginning of the 1970s neither the popular forces nor their vanguard organizations (much less the social scientists of the region) could have predicted the extent of the crisis that would shake Central America so profoundly during ensuing years. But even if those forces had been able to understand events as they occurred, that understanding would not have enabled them to either control or foresee the events that followed.

And it is precisely the unexpected, the unforeseen, that constitutes the uniqueness of a revolutionary process. Throughout the 1970s— sometimes imperceptibly, often through social protest movements—a situation emerged that was increasingly characterized by a loss of control over the popular sectors. Its corollary was the growing delegitimization of power.

The outstanding feature of recent years has thus been the accumulation of unforeseen events, moving in contradictory and haphazard directions, and marked by an interminable chain of failures. The lesson of all those years, nevertheless, is that defeat represents the deceptive, inevitable pause before victory.

Defeat here refers not merely to a collapse in the face of superior power but, more appropriately, to the temporary loss of a chosen course of action. This happened, for example, in Guatemala, where the guerrillas had been almost completely destroyed by the end of the 1960s. Their struggle had begun following the military coup of March 1963, when the army as an institution had assumed control of the state for the first time. The military thereby clumsily eliminated a historic opportunity to stabilize counterrevolutionary power through the prudent and reformist government that Juan José Arévalo—the obvious winner had the elections taken place—would have attempted to organize.

Similarly, in El Salvador, a broad coalition of Christian Democrats, Social Democrats, and Communists were clear winners of the February 20, 1972, presidential elections.[2] But once again the dominant interests of the coffee-based bourgeoisie and the army—in control since 1932— resorted to fraud. This was an open act of force, of arbitrariness backed by military violence. It was also the last opportunity to initiate a period of civilian government whose moderate character was assured by the hegemony of the Christian Democratic party within the Unión Nacional Opositora.

The Frente Sandinista de Liberación Nacional (FSLN), founded in 1961, suffered a severe defeat at Pancasán in 1967, and its urban organization was almost liquidated in Managua in 1969. From then until its reorganization in 1974, the FSLN lived an obscure, "cellular" existence.

Meanwhile, in 1971, the Conservative party agreed to yet another electoral alliance with Somoza. That deal between the two corrupt traditional parties produced a new peak of dictatorial power. Only the social consequences of the 1972 earthquake, the persistence of the Sandinistas, and other well-known events permitted the end of Somocismo to appear plausible after 1978.

The experience of El Salvador constitutes an important landmark in a Central American countryside plagued by violence and the gradual consolidation of military dictatorship. In 1972, the alliance headed by José Napoleon Duarte—denied power via electoral fraud—constituted a decisive test of the survival capabilities of a system that showed no visible signs of weakening.

That alliance was the opportunity for a moderate group of forces, with a Kennedy-style reformist program and broad popular support, to open the road toward a democratization of the political structure. Had it remained in power, it would have represented a successful example of the project of "democratic reconstitution with development" then being advanced by various groups.

New political forces had appeared in the very moment that popular movements were suffering a string of defeats. Those new forces were struggling for a similar program by different means. They formed an option that attempted to avoid both the revolutionary Left's failures and the excesses of conservative power. The government of José Figueres in Costa Rica (1970–1974) was an example of the realization of that "third option." In contrast, moderate social forces were weak in Guatemala and Nicaragua.

Meanwhile the new political forces suffered yet another setback in El Salvador, where a process of gradual political hardening, characterized by a militarized state apparatus, was under way. By the mid-1970s, that third force had dissolved irreparably, with part of it joining the ranks of the insurgency.

Honduras presented a somewhat different picture, marked by a new type of campesino movement that asserted itself in the early 1970s by means of violent actions and land seizures. In Honduras, therefore, the landowners had become the ones who had to live precariously. An attempt to stabilize the situation was frustrated in 1972 when a civilian coalition government headed by Ramón Cruz was overthrown in a military coup headed by Oswaldo López Arellano. The military—whose prestige had risen little since the "war" with El Salvador in 1969—

were able to move within a reformist space only briefly. Their meager credibility—soon exhausted—brought little more than the initiation of an agrarian reform program. Nevertheless, popular forces were not subjected to persecution, as was the case in the neighboring countries.

It must be recognized that in the region as a whole—with the exception of Costa Rica—moderate political forces had no real opportunity to establish themselves as alternatives to authoritarian governments openly backed by the United States. Moreover, those moderate forces themselves lacked effectiveness and were paralyzed more by fear of revolution than by military repression.

In any case, there were many examples of those forces: "Arevalismo" and the Revolutionary and Christian Democratic parties of Guatemala; the Christian Democrats and their former allies of 1972 in El Salvador; the anti-Somoza Conservative party factions as well as Social Christian and Liberal party groups in Nicaragua.

In the long run, however, these moderate forces perceived the popular sectors as little more than an auxiliary force for their own struggles. They always feared, for example, the autonomous and radical behavior of the working class. When push came to shove, they repeatedly chose to make deals with the most reactionary sectors of the bourgeoisie, with the military, and with imperialism.

Regardless of the many opportunities, then, this was the period in which the problematic process of creating a democratic alternative was crushed in the political sphere. That democratic option—implying the partial integration of popular sectors—proved again and again to be difficult, if not impossible.

The decade of the 1970s was a critical one in the evolution of Central American social conflicts. It is not possible to summarize those conflicts one by one. However, during those years of internal crisis gestation, the dominated classes neither submitted nor compromised despite the adversity they encountered.

For example, the strikes of both Aceros S.A. in 1967 and ANDES (National Association of Salvadoran Educators) in 1965 and 1972 expanded into general strikes, which were brutally repressed. The city of San Salvador—a melting pot of the urban masses and of those displaced from the countryside—had become the chosen ground of conflict.

In Guatemala, too, social struggles and labor organizations grew after 1974, with their actions also focused on urban centers. The 1977 Miners' March from the town of Ixtahuacan to the capital mobilized over 300,000 people. Then came the general strike of August 1978—ignited by bus fare hikes—which represented the most significant moment of mass mobilization up to that time.

In Nicaragua, construction, hospital, and factory workers were successful in pressing their demands through a series of strikes that began in 1973. In all of those urban confrontations—as in El Salvador and Guatemala—the student movement was very active, and many demonstrations were met by harsh military repression.

From 1978 onward, the critical factors described above were present throughout Central America. Their potential was almost as great as their unpredictability. What took place constituted a sequence of "unforeseen" events that, in any case, had long been brewing. As of 1978 the old Roman belief concerning war and religion—that the gods always take the side of the largest battalions—was no longer valid.

What should not be misinterpreted is the superficial simultaneity of the diverse national crises. The regional perspective presented here is not meant to contradict the essentially national nature of those conflicts nor the particular ways in which they evolved. In each of the three countries under consideration, the origins of the conflict date back some time.

In Guatemala, for example, the conflict began with the fall of Arbenz and the National Revolutionary experience in 1954. With El Salvador one must go back to the massacre of campesinos in 1932 and review forty-five years of military rule. In Nicaragua the terms of conflict had been set in 1937, when the dictatorial dynasty of Somoza effectively meant a prolongation of North American military intervention.

That simultaneity, therefore, is varied, with different key moments of crisis. Only the blindness that accompanies bad faith could found a strategy on the so-called domino theory. But there is no doubt that one victory feeds another. What the several crises have in common is a social dynamic no longer determined by confrontation between competing bourgeois factions, but rather between opposing classes. In other words, the contemporary crises are occurring at a level qualitatively different from those of an earlier era.

Setting the Stage

The peculiarities of Central American society form the framework of the process analyzed here. Those peculiarities are a result of the historical evolution of the region's bourgeois society, of the state, and above all, of its social classes. Explanations of the crisis that blame insoluble economic problems—seeing the agitated surface of the political structure as nothing more than a reflection of those economic determinants—are clearly inadequate.

Therefore the notion of a "degraded" capitalism, while probably useful at some other level of analysis, has no utility here. It would be a gross oversimplification to attribute to the state-political sphere the status of a more or less sophisticated reflection of the economy, ultimately determined by the evolution of that economy. A particular set of historical conditions framing the overall process of capitalist development must be examined.

The confusions created by this approach tend to reveal themselves in Siamese twin fashion. On one side, the crisis is said to be one of "maturity," caused by societal decomposition and the accompanying accumulation of problems. Facing that breakdown is the inevitable revolt of the poor, the "revenge of those who seek bread," the subversion of those humble folk produced in droves by the system.

In order to characterize the stage upon which the conflict occurs, it is necessary to suggest some hypotheses and to establish some facts. To begin with, since the end of World War II—and particularly during the 1960s and 1970s—Central America experienced its most important period of economic growth and differentiation. Crises and stagnation were not entirely absent, but in a medium-range vision that growth was significant. Most importantly, it was superior to that attained during previous periods. Had these social and economic changes—in effect, a deepening of capitalism—not taken place, some of the events that now form part of the explanation probably would not have occurred.

In fact, the specifically economic character of the Central American crisis has a triple explanation. First, it is the consequence of the development of the contemporary period rather than of stagnation. Second, it is in part a crisis of external origin. And finally, it has been sharpened by the effects of the most recent political conflicts.

In the postwar period, the economic system seemed to split as a result of external dependency, with the old agro-export model giving way to the model of internally oriented development stimulated by the Central American Common Market. With state support, a considerable effort to push import substitution industrialization was mounted simultaneously with the diversification of the agricultural sector. The two processes, because of state policies—which affected the distribution of resources—and the differing final destinations of the products, occurred independently of one another.

A notable aspect of this dual mechanism of capital accumulation is that it was not sponsored by different and therefore conflicting social classes. Instead, local family-centered economic groups and foreign capital controlled the process. They in turn depended on external demand and are today subjected to the whims of international finance capital.

Central American society remained agrarian. Important growth and new products—cotton, sugar, meat—appeared, but the growth was based on renewed processes of land concentration, extensive cultivation, and the takeover of the best lands. Within the agrarian sector, export production attained high levels of productivity while that of food crops for the internal market remained extremely low. The economy produced hard currency but little food while the agrarian frontier was nearly exhausted and the population more than doubled.

In short, the primary sector's contribution to the functioning of the system was rather contradictory. It proved to be incapable of either generating employment or increasing income levels. As a consequence, 40 percent of the population was placed at the threshold of absolute poverty. The crisis of the historically debt-ridden agricultural sector worsened, but in a radically different context. The effects of processes as varied as increasing fertilizer use and the penetration of finance capital partially destroyed traditional forms of subsistence farming.

These new factors, coupled with the increasing use of money at all levels of agrarian exchange, made the consumption patterns of the rural population even more vulnerable. Here it should be recalled that the Central American economies had not experienced inflationary trends during the entire postwar period preceding the second moment of the international crisis in 1974–1975. Inflation was a new and unknown phenomenon in the region, whose countries had long enjoyed monetary stability. It arose as a consequence of expanded capitalist relations throughout the whole of society.

This ensemble of factors had a profoundly favorable effect on the accumulation of capital. That accumulation took place partly via the extraction of absolute surplus value and partly through increases in productivity that bore no relation to workers' wage levels. In other words, social differences only increased with economic growth. The mechanisms of accumulation in the new industrial sector also became a major focus for the concentration of wealth. Scarce capital resources were placed definitively in the hands of the few, with the added benefit of excessive state protection. This partly explains weaknesses inherent in the project of regional economic integration that have now become manifest. Although excessive industrial protectionism certainly did not harm export agriculture, in an indirect manner it did damage the artisan sector (both urban and rural), basic food producers, and in general, those groups whose capacity for organization and defense of salary levels was very low.

The state always appeared at the center of this network of contradictory pathways: All roads led to it whenever the bourgeoisie was involved. Indeed the latter were able to take advantage of concentrated banking capital, restricted access to public credit, favorable interest rates, manipulated tariff regulations, tax exemption policies, and the repression of the labor movement. It all added up to permanent subsidies to capital at the expense of labor and at levels even higher than those of most Latin American societies.

This type of political capitalism has turned the state and bureaucratic favors into particularly critical features of the present crisis. In the process, the bourgeoisie was converted into a class of diminished social importance and extreme functional concentration. In other words, by virtue of its absolute control of political power, the bourgeoisie became monopolistic owners of the entirety of each country's productive forces.

The policy dilemma between growth and distribution had become hypocritical within this context. This was not so much because it constituted an inherent feature of capitalist growth, but rather because the distribution of wealth is essentially a political problem. It depends on the capacity of the working class for organization and struggle, as well as the effectiveness of independent leadership in the defense of wage levels and other union demands. Those efforts have been relentlessly repressed throughout the past twenty-five years.

Favors and repression have necessarily been linked directly to the state, whose policies have never abandoned a bizarre neoliberal inspiration. Those policies have not been examples of classical economic liberalism because interventions actively favored both foreign and national capital. This explains the formation of dominant classes that were well protected on all sides: from sectoral competition, from contradictions between agriculture and industry, and from workers' wage demands.

As an extension of this, the process of Central American economic integration was carried out without a social expansion of the market, that is, without augmenting the income level of the lower-class majority. In addition, external financing was (and continues to be) sought in order to avoid fiscal and other reforms. The style of growth that was promoted increased both the quantity and quality of social differences. As a consequence, social polarization not only increased but also became more visible.

However, this does not necessarily mean that the model has been exhausted, though the cumulative nature of that model seems to indicate that limits may already have been reached at the level of the internal market.

In any case, the growing instability of the regional market seems unavoidable. Part of the reason for that assertion lies with international causes of the crisis: Imperialism has been, and will surely continue to be, responsible for a number of the basic contradictions. Political conflicts complete an economic picture that is conclusively favorable to the further development of the crisis.

The Interbourgeois Crisis

As the French revolution of 1848 and many other international experiences have demonstrated, the dominated classes can take advantage of crises provoked by the bourgeoisie itself. "The name linked with the beginning of the revolution will never be inscribed in banners raised on the day of victory," wrote Marx. "Revolutions must get their entry ticket from within the official theatre of the ruling classes themselves."[3]

The Central American revolutionary movement was born within the context of an interbourgeois crisis, formed in each country at a different moment and responding to a cadence imposed by unresolved contradictions. As it unfolded during the 1970s, the movement was confronted, not by a united and solid reactionary power, but rather by a situation that fed itself on a crisis of hegemony. In effect, the internal conflicts of the dominant classes sat precariously upon the same contradictions that gave birth to the ascendency of the masses.

Though the interbourgeois crisis did not have a single set of common origins, behind the diverse phenomena produced by that crisis lay a specific form of perpetuation or resolution of contradictions. Those contradictions arose from a combination of oligarchic domination and the critical early stages of bourgeois society.

The oligarchic component was related more to a style of political-ideological leadership typical of the agrarian classes than to the form of the state and the development of its physical apparatus. That ideological style was based on the natural exclusion of the dominated and on an equating of narrow elite interests with those of the nation in general. The nation was constructed as a special, unique body, nourished by a culture of exclusion. Oligarchical conflicts were therefore resolved in an incomplete manner and now lie superimposed upon the contemporary crisis of bourgeois regime consolidation.

The bourgeoisie had never been a homogeneous class and became even less so during the brief moments of expansion in Central America after the 1950s. Its internal differentiation was the inevitable result of the concentrated and inharmonious development of capitalism.[4] That differentiation was all the more accentuated in societies with an agrarian base, where the expansion of capitalist relations of production had been stimulated from abroad.

Internally, the interbourgeois crisis was a product of the ways in which relationships between factions of the dominant classes—as well as between those factions and the state—were modified. Obviously, the shape of those relations was also affected by international capital. At the same time, neither bourgeois modernization nor possibilities for accumulating wealth and capital were distributed equally across the board. Those processes were determined by new relations with the external market and by the control of political power. Struggles over that control have been a constant feature of relations among right-wing groups and parties.

The advances of capital in agriculture after 1950, stimulated by external demand, pushed back the outmoded latifundium. A new agricultural bourgeoisie therefore appeared, mechanized and open to new market possibilities.

As has already been mentioned, the project of Central American economic integration—based on the forced substitution of imported consumer goods—created other elements of differentiation. But it was the political conditions required in order to expand the bases of capitalist accumulation and reproduction that produced readjustments of economic interests. Those conditions, ultimately linked to external factors, were expressed as tensions and struggles either with or within the state. It was there, rather than in the marketplace where they originated, that resolutions were sought. Interbourgeois competition had thereby been transformed into an institutional crisis.

In Guatemala, national revolutionary politics and mass mobilization created a transitory unification of the bourgeoisie—based on fear— which lasted until 1954. But acrimonious conflicts at the apex of power appeared immediately after the fall of Arbenz. As in other countries, they were generally expressed indirectly as military conspiracies, barrack coups, and divisions within the army. Bourgeois factions used the military putsch to advance their interests and to resolve their differences. Only recently has the conflict become one directly affected by the interests of the armed forces themselves.

In El Salvador the conflicts appeared late because of the particular nature of the bourgeoisie: a *grande bourgeoisie*, limited in number, under the indisputable hegemony of the coffee growers. But those conflicts had come into the open by 1960, when interbourgeois disputes provoked the downfall of the José María Lemus government. They reemerged in 1976, in response to the agrarian policies of the Arturo Molina military dictatorship, and again in 1979 with the ascendancy and victories of the popular movement.

Only in Nicaragua did the various bourgeois groups maintain a constant rupture, which became definitive after 1975. The interbourgeois conflict was essentially an economic rivalry between three well-known factions: the Somoza Group, the Bank of America Group (with Conservative party ties), and the Bank of Nicaragua Group (with Liberal party ties). That competition, not surprisingly, took place at the level of political parties as well.

The economic differentiation of classes, which had been taking place throughout the region since the immediate postwar period, was exposed by the economic crisis of 1974–1975. The popular movement grew in the face of a bourgeoisie stung by international recession. Thus the general crisis of the system blended with the particular, national crises of each bourgeoisie.

Here there is a danger of exaggerating, in an abstract sense, the gravity of the interbourgeois crisis. In fact it remained a contradiction that was not fundamentally antagonistic and could therefore be resolved in different ways depending on the real popular threat.

In Nicaragua, armed insurrection resolved interbourgeois disputes in a revolutionary way by preventing the mediated compromise desperately sought by U.S. imperialism and various business groups. In the case of Guatemala, popular mobilization has taken place during a period of prolonged counterrevolutionary actions. That period has strengthened the bourgeois-military axis, maintaining the possibility of a reactionary solution to the interbourgeois crisis. In El Salvador, equidistant from the other two experiences, popular insurrection only managed to activate the interbourgeois crisis, provoking a major schism in October 1979. However since then—and above all since the outbreak of open civil war in January 1980—the reformist solution has been more or less paralyzed.

Rather than being a mirror merely reflecting events taking place around it, the state became the center stage of conflict. There the bourgeoisie disguised its role as a historical actor beneath the anonymity of institutional forces, and only an analysis of the political game could reveal the identity of the various factions. But as a result, interbourgeois disputes provoked institutional earthquakes.

Obviously the state is something more than "the state of the bourgeoisie," but it is also something less than "the state of all." The bourgeoisie proceeded in the way it did because it saw the state as a means of achieving class unity. That goal became a possibility in the region's backward societies, where a diminished margin of relative autonomy placed the state at the disposition of the most powerful class. In this manner, the state became the terrain upon which the *dominant* social forces constituted themselves politically. At the same time, the means chosen by the *dominated* social forces was completely different: the political party, the popular movement.

The interbourgeois crisis clearly did not facilitate the formation of democratic participatory institutions, though their marked absence in the political life of Central America should not be attributed to that cause alone. Dictatorship, however, was clearly an appropriate means of resolving the contradictions of capitalist growth appearing within the bourgeoisie itself. The ongoing internal recomposition and the difficulties encountered in preserving the old system of alliances[5] necessitated a strong apparatus of political control.

The regional interbourgeois crisis had two other outstanding features. First of all, the bourgeoisie lacked organizations of its own and failed to produce leaders that could head multiclass movements of any real consequence. An important missing element was therefore the organic articulation of bourgeois political interests, a process shaped through the exercise of power.

Although the current political crisis has clearly been a crisis of all forms of party organization, the left-wing forces have been the ones most affected. Right-wing parties have not suffered to a like degree because they have never existed as genuine political parties. The bourgeoisie did not need party channels of mediation and participation because its representation within the state was both direct and total. Only the liberal-democratic power game requires parties.

There were exceptions of course. In Guatemala, the extreme Right managed to consolidate the Movimiento de Liberación Nacional, dubbed the "party of violence" by its leader, Sandoval Alarcón. In Nicaragua, the commercial "aristocracy"—later transformed into a commercial and financial elite—succeeded in preserving a miniscule but respected Conservative party.

Perhaps most characteristic was the Partido Liberación Nacional of Costa Rica—the true social-democratic expression of a society in which the working class was far from being a majority of the population. The rest were multiclass parties led by middle-class members. They were little more than transitory electoral machines with ambiguous programs that did not express the political self-identification of the bourgeoisie.

The second important feature of the interbourgeois crisis was an absence of effective ideological discourse of a bourgeois nature, capable of providing a base for hegemonic leadership. Indeed the Central American bourgeoisie was not only a political orphan in terms of its failure to form a significant political party and to produce an indisputable national leader. Worse yet, it turned to that most impoverished of ideological defenses—anticommunism—as justification for its rule and as pretext for repression. The vacuousness of that ideology lay in the fact that its defense of the status quo was based on a negation. It could not offer an alternative doctrine, much less present an ideological and intellectual statement of bourgeois beliefs and principles.

Finally, the importance of the interbourgeois crisis changed perceptibly in the 1970s when the army emerged as the pivot of an authoritarian structure that seemed momentarily to seal off internal disputes. The primary role of those disputes became the degree to which they conditioned relations between the bourgeoisie and the dominated classes. In effect, the counterrevolutionary bourgeoisie suffered the simultaneous debilitating effects of internal division and open conflict with the lower classes.

Therefore, the political crisis in Central America is not merely an expression of secondary contradictions that have yet to be resolved within the dominant class. Rather, it is an open class struggle that questions the very foundations of bourgeois domination.

The Character of the Popular Presence

There is no doubt that a new period in the ascendancy of popular struggles has begun throughout Latin America. Since 1975, the mobilization of the working class and the campesinos has been expressed through both a clearer definition of their interests and a new type of radicalism marked by a more developed sense of autonomy. Central America clearly took part in this profound renovation of social conflict. But from its very origins, the popular presence in the region had particular features that help explain its role in the present crisis.

For a long time the dominated social sectors only occasionally tested their capacity to confront bourgeois power directly. Social protest movements remained little more than a threat. There were other important political processes in the postwar period—great social movements against dictatorships—but their leadership did not emerge from the popular sectors, and they opted for the peaceful political tactics of the generalized civil strike. The dictatorships of Ubico, Hernández Martínez, Carías Andino, and Somoza were all either checked or ended by movements of that kind.

And other significant civilian movements did develop—such as those of spring 1962 in Guatemala, and the general strike in 1960 against Colonel Lemus in El Salvador. Then, in 1967, Nicaraguans Fernando Agüero and Pedro Joaquín Chamorro led a violent Conservative party offensive against the Somoza dictatorship.

There were moments in which popular protest went beyond an amorphous and spontaneous character, when the movement's political conduct tended to become more homogeneous. During the 1970s, that kind of mass protest became ever more possible.

Here it should be recognized that the "mass" as a social subject is only a manner of articulating diverse social interests. Within it, particular group-wide interests can achieve specific expression. What characterized the new stage was the acquisition of more precise concepts of unified popular action, despite the overall heterogeneity as well as the traditional practices of many social groups involved. Tendencies toward disorga-

nization, atomization of protest, and short-term combativity were gradually being overcome.

It is well known that the fate of the popular classes is the product
of a two-edged sword. On one side are the dominance and exploitation
by the upper classes; on the other, the strength of the popular classes'
own efforts. Historically, external influences have been decisive, and the
dominated have tended to express ambiguous desires, thereby facilitating
the "victories" of others. Today, however, the popular classes on the
whole define their actions as steps toward the realization of their own
historic goals; they are prepared to take chances as agents of their own
destiny.

Here, then, are some of the most profound aspects of the crisis: new
forms of participation, the changing essence of the will to protest, violent
response to violence, and—what may be the most important of all—
the increasing congruence between class interests and class actions among
the urban and rural proletariat at the center of the conflict. This clearly
applies more to the cases of Guatemala and El Salvador than to that
of Nicaragua.

In the immediate postwar period, the working-class movement and
popular struggles in general tended to fuse into expressions of generic
dissatisfaction that blurred their objectives as well as the profile of the
enemy. The weaknesses of that stage were in turn related to the absence
of an organic tradition. More specifically, the weight of the artisan sector,
of the traditional peasant, and of a demobilizing culture—which confined
political activity to the propertied classes—served to limit the movement's
potential. In any case, several important characteristics of the popular
movement should be made more explicit. The following traits have been
present since World War II, but have become increasingly significant
over the past fifteen years.

1. When the working-class and campesino movements organized
themselves, they did so autonomously, independent of state control and
of employer support. Except for a few fleeting experiences of union
leaderships at the service of the bourgeoisie—too brief to produce
capitulation or long-term compromise—working-class action was marked
by opposition to the political order and, consequently, by its semilegal
nature. That opposition provoked the intolerance of the bourgeoisie as
well as what by then had become more or less inevitable police repression.

Why was the Central American bourgeoisie, despite multiple possibilities of co-optation—through the church, imperialist labor organizations, and corruption—unable to establish even partial control over
the working-class and campesino organizations? Whether due to the
state's weakness or to lower-class virtue, the fact is that bourgeois politics

always found it difficult—when, indeed, it even bothered trying—to organize the ideological domination of the working class.

Is this the case of a bourgeoisie that did not have time to consolidate itself through a populist alliance? Or was that consolidation sought instead via authoritarian control over any reformist flirtation? Whatever the case may be, working-class organization exhibited an independent character that the bourgeoisie proved to be incapable of controlling. This led to the outlawing and violent repression of social conflict, on the one hand, and the search for political democracy, on the other. That search became a working-class demand of primary importance. Both factors must be recalled in any analysis of the current crisis.

2. Most likely as a consequence of the factors outlined above, the union movement was often "illegal," but only to the extent that the political order could not afford to legalize it or was unwilling to risk assimilation.

The popular movement was born in opposition and tended to grow clandestinely. No reformist practice was able to prosper, for basic social conflicts remained unresolved, and initiatives to incorporate lower-class demands were not allowed to proceed in a normal and predictable fashion. Even before the present crisis, anything deemed "popular" had become suspect, attracting repression as a guarantor of control.

3. In Central America, the impossibility of a social pact of the type repeatedly attempted in South America contributed to an aspect of the conflict that might be labeled "antipopulism." This was no doubt the product of the unresolved relationship between the oligarchic character of political domination and the evolving sphere of capitalist relations.

At the same time, social protest began to overflow the limits imposed by its atomized, corporatist origins and rapidly acquired a political dimension. During the 1970s even the most modest union demands were frequently raised in an uncompromising manner, thereby posing a threat to the existing order. Local union conflict rapidly deteriorated into political conflicts of national dimension largely because of an absense of bourgeois means of mediation, such as mass parties, co-opted unions, and populist ideologies. Demands limited to individual unions were usually abandoned, perhaps more as a result of bourgeois intolerance and the repressive response than of class consciousness.

In any case, the popular sectors had begun to take shape behind a new type of national-popular experience. Goals and action had become revolutionary. Many examples of the immediate polarization of student demands, of conflict in factories, or of street protests can be given. There were times when all of them, upon being repressed, converted limited corporatist demands into universal and national protests that affected the power of the state. On occasion they provoked the resignation of a chief of police, or an interior minister, or of the president of the republic himself.

In sum, the former organic-ideological backwardness—which was nearing its end in the 1970s—seemed to be compensated by a combativity that went well beyond questions of salary and food demands. There was a contradictory process at work within these direct confrontations with the system, produced by a situation of backwardness. Failures only stimulated resistance, and from the inequality of force emerged a strengthened—rather than a weakened—class experience. Thus the current revolutionary movement in Central America was born of defeat, not of domestication. It is the corresponding tenacity of the popular, collective will that has checkmated the Central American bourgeoisie.

The post-1975 revolutionary process has new characteristics that developed from the preceding features. There are ruptures that represent the triumph of subjective factors, while they are also reinforced by the continuity of a sustained objective tradition. The upshot of it all is a new kind of popular presence that expresses itself in new political and ideological constructs, new historical actors, and new forms of organized protest.

First, it is noteworthy that university and high school students were gradually replaced as the principal subjects of political protest. They had played a fundamental role in earlier democratic struggles, but their relative importance diminished vis-à-vis other sectors engaged in the popular movement. Schools and universities were producing numerous effective militants and political activists precisely because they had moved beyond their student status.

Second, it is important to point out the failure of left-wing parties, which were unable to organize and lead the popular struggles. This is particularly important with reference to the oldest ones, the Communist parties. Though long the sole representatives of the working class and the campesinos, and though fully experienced in clandestine work—as well as continual victims of brutal state repression—they were never able to translate their ideological underpinnings into vanguard action. Perhaps their fundamental mistake was to yield, in differing degrees, to the leadership role of the bourgeoisie in its project of liberal-democratic revolution. It was a historical error that has led to more than one defeat.

Paradoxically, the tragedy of those parties was that they came to know the landowning oligarchy before they did the bourgeoisie, and consequently they exaggerated the latter's role. Their stage-based conception of social development and revolution led them to overlook the interconnections between the landed elite and the bourgeoisie, rather than alerting them to distinct forms of hegemony and alliance that characterized different periods. Communist party policies, derived from theory, were inappropriate for the region's specific reality. Thus the unforeseen arrival of a new revolutionary crisis—requiring new class alignments—left them politically and militarily disarmed.

It is not possible here to enter into a detailed review of the different national experiences of the various Communist parties. But after 1960 the Guatemalan Labor party (PGT) accepted the armed struggle as the fundamental form of class struggle and dedicated itself to all the tenets of Guevarist *foquismo* prevalent in that period. The PGT emerged almost completely liquidated from that experience.

The Communist party of El Salvador, always very close to the urban masses, joined the Revolutionary Coordinator of the Masses (CRM) and later became part of both the Farabundo Martí National Liberation Front (FMLN) and the United Revolutionary Directorate (DRU).

The anti-Somoza stance of the two weak socialist parties of Nicaragua induced them to join the Democratic Liberation Union (UDEL)—under the bourgeois leadership headed by Pedro Joaquín Chamorro—in 1974. Today one of those parties continues to mount a worker-oriented opposition that is more backward than revolutionary.

Despite the above qualifications, it must be recognized that the Central American Communist parties have played a regional role of inestimable importance. Particularly in Guatemala and El Salvador, almost every significant revolutionary organization and militant has origins in one of those parties. The current political-military organizations in those countries therefore have common parentage and even the FSLN relied on the "transfer" of valuable militants from the two Nicaraguan socialist parties.

Are protest and struggle organized from a class position (that is, union, party) or centered in the popular, mass movements themselves? The question is a critical one for the development of class consciousness, in order to supersede a merely "instinctive" level of protest. There is no longer any doubt that confrontation has been activated directly by the social movements rather than being directed by political parties. But the substitution of the party by the movement requires a more rigorous analysis. It emerged not as a degradation of the organic structure, as Leninist thought would suggest, but rather from the difficulty of adapting that structure rapidly enough to the demands of the struggle. Therefore a functional solution based within the political structure—but responding to the exigencies of the military struggle—was not possible.

The focus turns briefly now to an examination of the character of both the new forms of organization and the new subjects of action. Organizations arose or reconstituted themselves through the self-critical appraisal of two types of experience: the impotence of the party, and the defeat of the guerrilla *foco*. The separation between the two in the

1960s was costly, with a mass movement led by one group and an insurrectionary struggle by another. The divorce was both sharp and bloody.

Today, the political-military organizations—a term that in itself underlines their dual unity—have taken this experience into account. They represent a reconciliation reached through concrete experience, an original and productive combination of economic, political, and armed struggle. That unity is consequently reflected in new links established between the unions, the political leadership, and the guerrilla groups.

But of course each national experience is unique. In Guatemala, the FAR (Rebel Armed Forces) has had a strong influence in the labor movement; ORPA (Revolutionary Organization of the People in Arms), in contrast, has been active almost exclusively in rural areas, particularly those populated by Indian campesinos; and the EGP (Guerrilla Army of the Poor)—probably the most experienced—has carried out an effective multiple strategy. They are all guided by the precept that mass struggle must precede successful armed struggle on a national scale. Admittedly, however, they do in some ways follow the model that creates one army in order to defeat another.

In El Salvador the experience has been quite different, though also marked by a concern for developing all possible forms of confrontation with imagination and audacity. In some cases guerrilla groups have worked with the masses and "produced" their own popular labor front. In others they have penetrated the already existing working-class movement and contributed to its reinforcement. Finally, guerrilla groups have worked in the countryside, solidly implanting themselves there.

The experience of the FSLN is equally diverse and probably better known. A long sequence of defeats—result of a strictly military conception in addition to other internal factors—provoked a division into three groups, which proceeded to carry out political work according to their own particular conceptions of the struggle. Those three "tendencies" included strategies centering on prolonged popular war in the countryside, on the one hand, and political work with the urban masses, on the other. Finally, the third group—called the "insurrectional tendency"— involved a coordination of the various methods of confrontation.

It was in Nicaragua, then—for the first time in Latin America—that all forms of struggle were effectively combined. In the countryside, revolutionary forces continued the tactics of guerrilla warfare and worked among the campesinos. In the cities they practiced all forms of insurrectionary political activism—in the neighborhoods as well as in the factories—calling for general strikes and collecting the support of middle-class groups and intellectuals. The FSLN was ultimately surrounded by a diversity of mass political organizations that provided extraordinary strength in the preparation of its military actions.

The popular organizations that came into being in the mid-to-late 1970s constituted a break with the traditional organizations and leadership of the masses. Of all those organizations, the FSLN came closest to the model of a popular army. During the final offensive it was capable of surrounding itself with mass organizations—that is, practically the entire population—from which it received unquestioning support. In the struggle against Somoza, in effect, the state was confronted by society.

Meanwhile the organizations that took shape in Guatemala and El Salvador constituted neither parties nor mere armies. Instead they were multiclass movements that adopted the transitional form of the "front," whose apex is the political-military structure and whose base is composed of a broad range of mass organizations not necessarily linked in any organic or ideological fashion.

What, then, is the national, popular principle of these truly original mass coalitions? Why are they able to recruit from all sectors of society? The transcendence of the traditional forms of participation implied a double movement—reflecting socioeconomic modifications within Central American society—which was expressed in new forms of organization and in the active presence of new participants.

Clearly the campesinos and the marginal sectors are the key new variables of the political equation. Their presence by itself destabilizes the system. The independent organizing of campesinos—who were no longer raising that most traditional of demands, a plot of land—constituted an immense act of civil disobedience. Even when carried out peacefully, the process of campesino participation was experienced as a profound crisis of authority.

In effect, only familiarity with the social and political backwardness of Central America enables one to appreciate the dimensions of the transformation of the campesinos into active participants in the revolutionary struggle. It has meant the end of fatalism and apocalyptic ideologies, obstacles that only revolutionary violence has been able to dismantle.

The popular struggles rose to a higher level after 1975 because violence became an immediate form of incorporation, while also constituting an equally immediate answer. The conflict thereby acquired unprecedented dimensions. The bourgeoisie correctly recognized that the very existence of mass organization in the countryside was a serious defeat, precisely because independent organization had appeared an impossible feat for so many years.

The campesinos had not overcome repression and control by traditional means, though certainly every method of control was attempted. In El

Salvador, for example, the bourgeoisie organized civil patrols (*patrullas cantonales*), the National Guard, the army, the police, and ORDEN. The latter was created to act as a political policing organization made up of "midlevel" campesinos. It was intended as a means of controlling the campesinos from within while repressing them from without.

Similarly, in Guatemala there were the military commissioners (*comisionados militares*) and in Nicaragua the *jueces de Mesta* (a medieval term referring to nobles who sat in judgment of commoners). Each case represented an extremely effective method of forcing campesinos to perform functions of military intelligence, espionage, and open repression against their own kind.

The armed struggle of the campesinos and marginal social groups bestowed on the confrontation a previously unequaled level of violence. The Sandinista militias—recruited among the urban unemployed—were the first to demonstrate the destructive potential of marginal groups. The Salvadoran popular forces have also been fortified by the participation of the marginalized sectors, in a society where they have long been a significant majority. That participation is increasingly rural as well as urban. The irruption itself, seen in historical context, was a new phenomenon only in terms of its character, which beforehand had never been sustained. Those uprisings had always been "anti–status quo," a fundamental and powerful force that often exploded spontaneously, of its own accord. On the one hand, organizing them was not difficult because violent responses were a natural extension of their own social existence. However, the Nicaraguan experience showed that it can be extremely difficult to channel their energies into constructive work— that is, deliberate political action—and to develop a socialist awareness among them.

Finally, none of what is being analyzed here can be explained without taking into account the crucial contribution of religious groups. Actually, a separate analysis of their role is called for—of the way in which Christian groups came to "discover" the reality of mass misery and exploitation, of the process that gave their religious ministry an increasingly popular content.

The "new" religion taught that loving one's reality was a prerequisite to understanding it, and that understanding was in turn a prerequisite to change.[6] Through that approach, the Christian "base communities"— formed by priests and lay workers of many different denominations— became direct protagonists of the popular struggle, fusing themselves with the masses.

The experiences of the radicalized religious movements led them to work out a decodification of the theological discourse of the traditional, hierarchical church. Their new message was political and ideological:

the theology of liberation. The resulting critique of the system strengthened Christian faith and renewed its tenets of "solidarity among all God's creatures." Once again, fellowship came to include the family next door, the exploited neighbor. By virtue of that transformation, the act of faith became fundamentally subversive within the framework of the traditional culture. It was a directly political act, disorganizing what had been preordained.

With the unification of the political and military organizations, a convergence of the dominated classes took place. It included even those who had been marginalized by a process of "nonexploitation." The coexistence of different forms of radical consciousness within the popular movement also appeared: classical Marxist thought, Jacobite rebelliousness, and petit bourgeois democratic radicalism. That radical ideological mix was also tempered by the sensitivities of left-wing Christians as well as the ingrained, pre-class-conscious hatred of the marginalized urban sectors, and—above all—of the indigenous Guatemalan ethnic groups.

This ensemble of social forces began to develop a clear profile through the struggle itself. Nonetheless, many real difficulties remain to be overcome before that unity can fuse the groups into a powerful organic front, worth more than the mere sum of its organizations. Only then will the movement become an authentic national vanguard.

In any case those classes that have been exploited by the system are finally—though amid some disorder—asserting themselves in a national sense. They are rising to present their own alternative to the past, writing their own popular version of national history, while giving it a political meaning that had long been denied.

The Crisis of the Counterrevolutionary State

For a long time the superficial appearances confounded analyses and strategies. Modifications of the power relations between classes were not perceived during the 1960s. At that time, everything seemed to point toward the constitution of the state of emergency; that is, to a political system confronted by crisis.

Like any other form of relation, this type of state is a "hybrid" because it emerges with the objective of solving a particular form of crisis. That crisis is the same one, of course, that has been analyzed—perhaps unsuccessfully—in the preceding sections. It can be summarized as the difficulties of hegemony within the power elite and in its relations with the popular masses.

States of emergency arise—and not necessarily in an extreme form— in order to stabilize a political order in crisis. In Central America, the recomposition of classes had been expressed within the state as a military dictatorship. The army was the only institution that could place itself at the center of the process. This was partly due to the inability of the different factions of the bourgeoisie to reach a stable agreement, but was above all a response to the uncontrolled irruption of the popular sectors.

The region's state of emergency took the form of a counterrevolutionary military dictatorship. It was the military presence—and nothing else—that gave meaning to the new character of the state. Although it is true that repression is a fundamental feature of any power relationship, in Central America the repressive apparatus reconstituted itself in a particular manner and occupied the central nucleus of the state, the epicenter of power.

Thus one institution developed the capacity to direct the entire state apparatus, becoming sole decisionmaker. In this manner, the equilibrium of power that normally constitutes the basis of liberal democracy was broken. However, that process integrated and unified the bourgeoisie through the temporary suppression of bourgeois contradictions.

From that moment on, the army, as caretaker of the state apparatus, began to act like the political party of the bourgeoisie. The divisions and conflicts within society that express a specific relationship between forces were thus reproduced—at times in a veiled manner—within the military itself. The state was still a bourgeois state, but its exceptional nature implied a crisis of representation, a crisis of the state as the expression of the general will. That crisis was clear in the contradiction implicit in the state's simultaneous role as neutralizer and representative of opposing interests.

But the counterrevolutionary state had little need for liberal-democratic rituals of expressing the general will, partly because it had arisen out of the bourgeoisie's incapacity to establish alliances. That state's internal recomposition made it more difficult either to preserve the old system of alliances or to establish a new one. Internal instability, in turn, reinforced the repressive character of the political order that had been created.

Military dictatorship first took shape in Guatemala with the coup d'état of March 30, 1963. That coup forestalled the election of Juan José Arévalo and placed the armed forces as an institution at the center of power. In El Salvador, military officers have run the government since the early 1930s, but it was the coup of January 25, 1961, that produced the definitive institutionalization of the army as an executive of state power.[7] In the case of Nicaragua, the Somozas' plebeian dynasty had long ensured its control with the direct support of a praetorian guard.

In all three cases, military dictatorship produced the following similar results:

1. They were regimes resting upon the systematic exercise of repression and after 1975 upon open, generalized terror.

2. Consequently, they were regimes that expressed a profound vaccuum of legitimacy that originated within the dominant groups and permeated all of society. Thus, the state was well armored, but weak.

3. They were regimes that no longer supported themselves with the institutions that traditionally produce consensus and the ritual of class representation. That meant devaluation of parliamentary functions, lack of respect for judicial organs, and uniformity of the right-wing press (the "respectable" way of destroying press freedom). They did no better with elections, whose fraudulent nature hardly provided the legitimation they desired. In sum, there was a total devaluation of all contemporary bourgeois-democratic forms.

Here was a state power that violated itself. The fact that it did not respect its own definition of legality vis-à-vis the dominated classes was less significant than its violations of that legality vis-à-vis members of its own class.

In Guatemala, for instance, the winner of the 1974 elections, General Efraín Ríos Montt, was cast aside by General Kjell Laugerud. And in El Salvador, General Carlos Humberto Romero was declared the winner of the 1977 electoral fraud against General Ernesto Claramount. These are only isolated examples; the crisis of confidence struck directly at the heart of petit bourgeois democratic formalities.

For a variety of reasons, the state lost its ability to control—and later, to disorganize—social struggles. The crisis of the state has now become a crisis of the entire society. It is being confronted within the context of gradual but inexorable gains for the masses—of political space, recognition, and influence—under the direction of political-military vanguards of Marxist orientation.

Thus a combination fatal to the bourgeois order has emerged. On the one hand, the objective conditions of an unjust socioeconomic structure remain. On the other hand, permanently postponed redress of all the problems engendered by that structure's long-term development has contributed to the emergence of popular organizations possessing the strength and courage necessary to give subjective expression to those objective conditions.

That combination—which represents a definitive victory for the subjective factors—explains both the nature of class confrontation and the rupture that led to the isolation of the military dictatorship, but does not explain the ultimate nature of the crisis. The essence of that crisis must be sought in the manner in which the rupture took placed within the state and the dominant class itself. For class contradictions are not produced outside the state. Rather, they crisscross it in all possible dimensions.

The policy of state terrorism, for example, is nothing more than a response to those contradictions, as inevitable as the bourgeoisie's "flight in advance."[8] By virtue of that flight, the Central American bourgeoisie's roots of domination came to lie outside rather than within the political space they sought to rule. That flight is also an illustration of how the bourgeoisie has acted without a sense of history, sacrificing its class existence to the needs of the moment.

The contradiction implicit in this analysis is that the bourgeoisie— by virtue of its monopolistic character, its concentrated control of wealth, and its association with foreign capital—constitutes a weak political force brought together within the state. Only in that way is there any sense to the dictum that asserts that the bourgeoisie is the subject of the state because its true character is revealed there. However, this leads to a consideration of the second part of that dictum: that the "nation" is the realm of the "people," for it is only there that the general will can be defined and expressed.

The bureaucratic apparatus of Somocismo defended itself entirely from its moorings in the state, without establishing political alliances. Meanwhile the bourgeoisies of the other countries appear to be increasingly alone, except for their external imperialist support.

Meanwhile, among the dominated sectors the opposite phenomenon has taken place. Indeed the popular offensive has come to consist of a broad front that occasionally defines itself as "the nation-in-movement." It was certainly that way in Nicaragua, and the revolutionary movement has had the same tendency in El Salvador, evident above all during the general strike of June 24–25, 1980. The Guatemalan revolutionary movement should also follow that course. Only if the popular forces can win over a qualitatively significant majority will victory be assured.

In summary, the state institutions that normally serve to maintain bourgeois domination—parliament, elections, organs of popular co-optation, and campesino pacification—have been thrust into crisis. The dominated sectors are testing the bourgeoisie's capacity for domination. And whereas the response, for many years, has been terror and violence, the dominated have now countered in kind.

If power is the capacity of a class to satisfy its immediate and long-run interests, the local bourgeoisie has foresaken its future and reneged on its responsibilities to the nation. The momentum of those attitudes sometimes resembles suicidal compulsions, though obviously that is not the case. However, the direction in which events are going clearly threatens the reproduction of the bourgeoisie as a class, and existing political forms hardly guarantee the system of social relations.

At the very least, then, the survival of the political system is not fully assured. For that reason, the state has openly transformed itself into a counterrevolutionary power, as daily occurrences in Guatemala and El Salvador have made clear. Understood in those terms, the crisis has thus become a crisis of the system itself.[9]

What Are the Popular Forces Fighting For?

Although ideological clarity is not a defining feature of the mass political-military movements in Central America, today's bloody process implies a break away from both reformism (action taken toward objectives contained or foreseen within the action itself) and voluntarism (the pursuit of objectives that go beyond the necessity and/or possibility of achieving them). The new strategy, then, transcends both right-wing opportunism and *gauchisme* (an outmoded kind of leftism). Whereas the former sought to postpone the inevitable rupture, the latter irresponsibly precipitated that rupture.

In the past, opportunism and *gauchisme* were responsible for the zigzagging course of the process, hastening its defeat. But the popular movement has taken lessons from both and now defines its goals in a more cautious manner. That is especially the case when it comes to abstract proclamations, acts of faith, or appeals to "reason" (a character trait long absent in the region).

Is there a revolutionary program capable of comprehending the magnitude of the crisis? The present revolutionary movement has been formed through the synthesis of many protest actions that almost inevitably turned into a critique of the existing system. It has defined itself through rejection. Alongside that act of conscience there has always been a self-proclamation of socialism as the ultimate goal. What kind of socialism? Has one form been clearly established as the inevitable model?

In Central America, where no bourgeois liberal-democratic culture rooted in historical traditions existed, the struggle for freedom and democracy became an act of rebellion. The bourgeoisie, because it expressed itself directly through the state, could afford to renege on democracy. The popular classes had to appropriate bourgeois banners, though in an ambiguous manner.

The struggle could not aim at the establishment of a bourgeois democracy, because that qualifier was not a natural feature of even bourgeois domination. In fact the experience of liberal and representative democracy after 1979 was a victory against the bourgeoisie. It was

produced by an active popular and—especially—working-class participation.

Here it should be recognized that universal suffrage has never been
a gratuitous concession anywhere. Rather, it has everywhere been a
conquest wrested after years of bloody struggle. Political regimes characterized by democracy, then, reflect a compromise between classes.

The first demand of the popular forces—of the programs of the
political-military organizations in particular—has been the establishment
of a democratic regime. The counterrevolutionary military dictatorship
has been Central America's "czarist autocracy." Confronted by a situation
similar to the one faced by the old Bolsheviks, the political-military
organizations' first task has become the overthrow of the autocracy in
order to build a fully participatory political structure. This has taken
shape as an antibourgeois demand because of the singular historical
conditions affecting the region and because of a process of capitalist
development unaccompanied by bourgeois political revolution.

The demand for a popular government proceeds from the conceptualization of democracy as participatory and free. In Central America
this has come to mean the substitution or defeat of one class by another.
A popular government would signify power for the victorious lower-
class majority. The consequences are in general terms foreseeable, but
they also depend on the particular conditions that would accompany
and condition that victory.

It must not be forgotten that in the Central American tradition factory
strikes degenerate into national strikes, and in a similar way individual
union demands are transformed via the magic of repression into generalized protest against the system. Social struggles become revolutions.
The latter, in turn, convert themselves into movements of national
liberation because the state and the bourgeoisie tend to rely more and
more exclusively on U.S. imperialism. Therefore anti-imperialism becomes
a defining characteristic of popular struggles opposing that bourgeoisie.

In any case, the revolutionary platform is not a finished product. It
has not been programmed in advance. In fact, unlike events of preceding
decades, the revolutionary process has evolved into an original and
creative affirmation of practice.[10] The Nicaraguan revolution has been
a fine example of that resolve, creating its own programmatic responses
through lessons drawn from experience.

Obviously, popular revolutionary theory did not arise out of nowhere.
But it has evolved in response to conditions of the society targeted for
destruction rather than the society to be created. In other words, there
is no set rationale for founding the society that is to follow, no ideology
defining the construction of a countermodel to the present system.

The Nicaraguan revolution—which is moving deeper toward a revolutionary restructuring of society at a pace that runs counter to the preferences of those who like simplified social models—has not fallen into the error of labeling itself beforehand. This is so, among other reasons, because the crisis of the bourgeois system of domination—the crisis of the bourgeoisie itself—has yet to be resolved. It is not a reflection of ambiguous objectives, for there can be no doubt whatsoever about the popular content of the Sandinista government or of its strategic strength.

Presently, the Central American revolution is neither bourgeois nor socialist. This is a result of objective conditions established by previous history, by imperialism, and by the international capitalist system. The programs of the political-military organizations of today, and of popular movements in general, are different from those of the 1960s. They are more mature, more realistic.

The democratic-revolutionary character of the current programs should be understood. They represent the end product of interaction between two revolutionary tendencies: unfinished bourgeois and incipient socialist.

But the character of the revolution itself must not be confused with the forms of struggle that guide its pursuit. Otherwise it might seem that socialism can only be proclaimed from the barrel of a gun. The armed struggle—the "savage" irruption of the masses—constitutes the heart of a process that seeks the ultimate construction of a democratic, popular, and revolutionary political system.

Among the many unfinished objectives of bourgeois domination in dependent societies of the imperialist epoch are the following: the conquest of national independence; the elimination of the latifundium; the establishment of democracy; the development of the productive forces; and the promotion of a popular culture.

It cannot really be said that the Central American bourgeoisie failed at these tasks, because they were never decisive for its existence as a class. Indeed there is no doubt that the execution of those tasks could only be carried out against, and in spite of, that class. But the coalition of social forces—formed primarily by the rural and urban working class, the campesinos, and the petit bourgeois sectors—does promise that possibility.

The programs of the popular movements lay out the first democratic-revolutionary stage in a more or less precise manner. The taking of power is viewed as a necessary condition for the accomplishment of that transition. Thereafter, the conquest of societal hegemony facilitates control of the state apparatus. The popular forces build a new majority through the gradual adhesion of formerly neutralized social forces. And thus begins the road toward socialism with freedom, toward a socialist democracy achieved without sacrificing any of those objectives so long denied by the old society. Every revolutionary process must attach itself to what is most progressive within its national tradition. Popular forces thus gain strength from the past, though their character is determined by the future.

The anti-imperialist figure of Augusto César Sandino in Nicaragua, of Augustín Farabundo Martí—assassinated by the Salvadoran oligarchy—and the reclaiming of the indigenous past in Guatemala are examples of that tradition. That is, the recuperation of each nation's history can produce a unique outcome to the crisis, ratifying the exceptional within each national process as well as the generic character of all authentic revolutions.

In any case, the lessons have been more modest. But the popular movement and its vanguard are acquiring the capacity to work out the historical as well as the democratic-revolutionary character of the revolutionary process. They have learned to combine diverse forms of mass struggle with armed confrontation. And finally, they have also understood—perhaps without ever reading Antonio Gramsci—that it is necessary to act with a mixture of intellectual pessimism and unbending optimism of the will.

The International Dimension

An explanation of the crisis in Central America can be completed only by incorporating the external actors into the analysis; that is, the international forces. Those actors—both old and new—acquire an extraordinary internal presence, thereby becoming equally decisive factors in the course toward a possible resolution of the conflicts.

Like few other regions of the world, Central America has been the object of other countries' foreign policy, and especially that of the United States. Particularly since the Spanish-American War of 1898, U.S. foreign policy has sustained an overwhelming influence, though U.S. activities in the region began somewhat earlier. The internal crises of Central America sooner or later reflect, in one way or another, the will of its powerful neighbor.

The crisis in Nicaragua revealed a new reality that did not derive from strictly national roots. Rather, it must be explained within the global context of a changing correlation of forces. The Nicaraguan crisis had an international dimension, with new relationships established among international interests contributing to the end of the Somoza dictatorship.

It was not that the internal conflict, led by the FSLN, became internationalized. What happened was that the popular struggle against the discredited regime occurred at a moment in which a combination of new influences was materializing in the region. This diverse set of influences translated a part of the internal conflict to the external plane. The international dimension of the crisis was characterized by a series of relationships and interests that took the shape of direct aid via arms and funding, diplomatic recognition, political pressures, and moral support, among others.

These influences can be grouped under two unequal headings: (1) North American policy, which was no longer guided by the "bipartisan approach" and which sought to gather support from other governments in the region through a traditional Pan-American perspective; and (2) the policies of other governments and international organizations, which resisted North American wishes with greater or lesser decisiveness, and to that extent acted as forces of opposition, containment, and rejection.

What the Nicaraguan crisis demonstrated was an erosion of U.S. hegemony in the region. It did not mean an end to U.S. omnipotence, but given that Central America had been the most secure region for imperialist policies—where the United States could count on its most trusted allies—the relative loss of influence was logically interpreted as a serious blow to U.S. designs on controlling the area. That loss of hegemony is important because of its potential effects on the outcome of the Salvadoran crisis, on the course of the increasingly virulent Guatemalan conflict, and naturally, on the ever more compromised fate of the Nicaraguan revolution.

It is necessary here to underline the special approach of the Carter administration toward the crisis in Central America. U.S. government policy under Carter was interested in supporting new social sectors whose reputations were unstained by human rights violations, corruption, and official violence. U.S. policymakers therefore set out in search of a "third force" that, in the case of Nicaragua, led to a rejection of both Sandinismo and Somocismo. Who, then?

A force that could avoid both the risk of Soviet penetration and the costs of maintaining old, discredited allies had to be found. This third force existed in Nicaragua and was made up of some of the organizations participating in UDEL (Democratic Liberation Union, a broad front led by members of the Conservative party) as well as a group of "notables"— that is, entrepreneurs and leaders of the traditional parties.

However, the Sandinista offensive destroyed any possibility of a resolution to the crisis based on the support of those sectors. The FSLN's strength made attempts at organizing a "viable" bourgeois democracy impossible in an area where neither electoral processes nor reformism had proven to be reliable.

The Reagan administration was oriented toward a return to the status quo ante. Its aim was not so much to guarantee a safe zone for investments[11] as it was to defend U.S. strategic interests.

In the obscure perspective of geopolitics there are no reliable allies, but in any case, old familiar allies are better. With them—the corrupt politicians and the bloodied military—there exists the possibility of restoring internal order. The costs include, where still possible, increased violations of human rights. And the "vision" that perspective implies is simplistic: again, a bipolar world in which the Soviet Union—through Cuba and now through Nicaragua—is attempting to expand toward new horizons.

Observing that political outlook and the events that it produces, forces of a new kind have begun operating today at the international level. They no longer believe in the possibility of finding the so-called third force—at any rate, not in Central America.

Here the influence of the Socialist International (SI) and of socialist and social-democratic governments from other regions—particularly Western Europe—is especially important. The motivating force behind the SI derives from its more sophisticated understanding of the world as well as its deep concern with the challenges to global peace posed by the policies of conservative U.S. Republicans at the helm of the Reagan administration.

The SI and some Latin American governments are advocating another type of viable democracy for a region where it has never existed. It is a democracy that can be constructed only after the defeat of the social and political forces that until now have made that construction impossible. Therefore a surprising amount of support—in the name of the right to self-determination—has been lent to the popular forces of Central America. That stress on free determination—the people's right to choose the regime they want and are capable of attaining—does not lead the SI to satanize guerrilla movements, but rather to encourage the democratic forces acting within popular movements.

The above is only a schematic presentation of how external actors have moved in relation to national conflicts that are not, in any case, beyond their purview. Clearly an internationalization of interest in the fate of democracy has taken place. And Central America is, at the moment, a place where that fate has come into play.

The region is important for the United States because it presents that nation an opportunity to recover from a loss of credibility suffered in its own backyard. For various Latin American governments and other international forces, it is important because in Central America a conception distinct from the politics of the great powers could either triumph or fail, and because by defending self-determination and democracy abroad the Latin American goverments secure those principles a bit more within their own borders.

Both of those tendencies act in support of internal forces already existing in the region. Thus, while the international dimension has demonstrated its importance in the crisis of Central American society, it is undoubtedly the social forces directly embroiled in conflict that will have the last word.

Notes

1. The analysis that follows refers particularly to Nicaragua, El Salvador, and Guatemala. The crisis now gripping Costa Rica is—for the time being—of a fiscal, economic nature, although it could eventually have political repercussions. The situation of Honduras is also distinct from the rest of the region, illustrating the difficulty of achieving equilibrium in a young democracy threatened from all sides.

2. Juan Hernández Pico et al., *El Salvador: año político 1971–72* (Publicaciones de la UCA, San Salvador, 1973). This is an extraordinary political document in terms of analysis and documentation. It describes events that surrounded the worst electoral fraud in the history of that country.

3. Fernando Claudin, "La superación del Estado Burgués," in *Teoría Socialista del Estado* (Editorial Mañana, S.A., Madrid, 1977), p. 132.

4. The differences generated within the bourgeoisie derived from the different functions of commercial, industrial, and finance capital. These three branches, or sectors, also experienced different patterns of development, diverse forms of association with foreign capital, and rivalries over credit and the formation of the financial sector.

5. In the postwar period, a rupture of the traditional alliance with the campesinos—"natural allies" of the bourgeoisie—took place. The agrarian bourgeoisie gradually lost the support of a dependable ally that had always been under its hegemonic control. Included within this context are the campesino rebellion of 1932 in El Salvador, the antilandowner response in Guatemala after 1955, and the massive peasant invasions in Honduras throughout the 1960s.

6. ALAI, *Coyunctura actual y vida cristiana* (ALAI, Año 4, No. 31, August 1980, Québec), p. 361.

7. The military proclamations that accompanied both coups seem to have been written by the same hand. The army, through internal deliberation—that is, "democratically"—becomes conscious of its role as guardian of order. And since it is the only institution that does not depend on the vote, that is, on "fickle plebeian practices," it takes over the entire state apparatus.

8. Data for 1978 indicate that deposits made in Swiss banks by Central American capitalists reached nine billion francs, an amount that would place Central America (as a whole) in third position among Latin American nations. Obviously, these bank deposits do not represent productive investment. That kind of investment is today located in Mexico, the United States, and other

financial centers. The source of this information, the Swiss National Bank, adds that the data do not include deposits in other institutions or investments in shares of Swiss companies.

9. U.S. economic intervention in El Salvador—greater even that its military aid—arose as a part of that process.

10. However, throughout the revolutionary processes in Central America there has existed a certain ideological backwardness vis-à-vis social movements. There has been neither debate nor theoretical confrontation, though numerous intellectuals are closely tied to the popular struggles.

11. It is clear that Central America has only geopolitical importance. U.S. investments in 1978 were estimated at $980 million, which represented 0.6 percent of its total foreign direct investment. Trade between the United States and the region amounted to $1.8 billion, which represented almost 1 percent of its total foreign trade. Other than petroleum, and possibly nickel from Guatemala, Central America possesses no resources vital to the U.S. economy.

5

The State Against Society: The Roots of the Nicaraguan Revolution

The Unfulfilled Tasks of the Bourgeoisie

No one seriously doubts that the fall of the Somoza dictatorship represented more than merely a popular victory. From whatever perspective one chooses to view them, the collapse of the military regime and the ensuing Sandinista victory were marked by both shortage and surplus. In both cases historical excess confronted insufficiency in a way that confirmed the absolute originality of Nicaragua's contemporary experience.

The analysis of two key factors is of primary importance here in order to understand that contemporary experience. The first involves an examination of the specific historical conditions behind the formation and operation of the Nicaraguan national state. The second point of analysis focuses on the construction of hegemony by a bourgeois class incapable of expressing itself other than within the limits imposed by a personalized dictatorship—particularly when that dictatorship embodies all the backward social conditions of the society that it dominates.

This latter point clearly helps to explain the proposition that whereas, on the one hand, the state was not *bourgeois* enough to resist change, on the other, neither was the popular uprising *proletarian* enough to establish a class-based orientation once the revolution was under way. That proposition might mistakenly be interpreted as implying a standoff between the past and the future. In fact, it was nothing more than a cruel act of revenge by the present, by a deformed capitalism that had established itself rather late in Nicaragua.

The dilemma of the bourgeoisie has arisen and sought resolution within a historical cycle marked by an extraordinary separation in space and time. To a certain degree, this is typical of dependent societies, for which the destruction of economic ties that pose obstacles to the full development of capitalism—particularly those ties of a structural nature— is generally accomplished in an incomplete manner. Moreover, the dependent economies' attainment of fundamental goals is rendered extremely difficult by inevitable interruptions—either sudden decline or general regression—of the long-term process.

The particular way in which precapitalist modes of production are interlaced with capitalist modes implanted from abroad constitutes a contradictory juxtaposition that is essential to any explanation of these societies. That juxtaposition—or more precisely, the interaction between the two modes—took the form of a prolonged transition that in itself represented the pattern adopted by capital movements. Those movements revealed capital's ability to adapt to adverse situations, to locate vantage points that would allow it to prosper at each juncture.

In Central America the cycle of so-called Liberal revolutions is generically associated with the beginning of a series of structural reforms. On the one hand, those reforms tended to favor the consolidation of large units of production—whether landed estates or otherwise—under the control of a small social group that took advantage of prevailing international conditions to create and develop a productive structure. On the other hand, the reforms included a set of measures of a superstructural nature that have been recognized as attempts to "modernize" the old terms of colonial domination. Those measures not only furthered the organization of the state apparatus, but also included laws and policies oriented toward foreign interests and the dominated classes at home.

Only through the misuse of terminology could one speak of a Liberal revolution in the sense of a bourgeois revolution. The divergence between the two becomes even greater when one refers to the historical experience of Nicaragua, where the stage marked by the establishment of agrarian and social bases of power by a Liberal bourgeoisie was not carried out "satisfactorily" in the typical Central American manner, that is, as it occurred in Guatemala, El Salvador, and Costa Rica.

The expansion of the coffee-exporting economy was relatively weak and in itself did not imply a transformation of the economic conditions already existing under the Conservative regime. That period was followed by the political gambit of the Liberal coffee-owning bourgeoisie—headed by General José Santos Zelaya—which was violently interrupted in 1909.

No one disputes the assertion that the coffee and commercial bourgeoisie were unable to prosper because of the low productivity of their

enterprises. But also important was the fact that North American intervention transformed—to say the least—the political existence of those
sectors. That vulnerability was related to their particular bourgeois
character, which had yet to mature at that point due to an insufficient
length of time for those sectors to exercise power. Thus the analysis of
Nicaragua differs from that of other national experiences, where an
examination of the state has revealed not only its bourgeois character
but also the bourgeois character of the dominant class itself.

Despite significant advances in the organization of the domestic order
under the Liberal government of General Zelaya, large landowner hegemony and the rule of the cattle estates only further solidified their
social and political importance. Neither coffee nor the creation of a
productive and commercial structure achieved any real alteration of the
overwhelmingly seignorial nature of local culture. The "oligarch as social
actor" continued to be a landlord, a monopolistic collector of other
people's land. And regardless of the size of the landowner's property,
production was small-scale and mercantile, weakly oriented toward
foreign trade.

The large landed estates—common throughout Central America—
were the product of the most ferocious forms of plunder. The height of
that process in Nicaragua followed the "war of the indigenous communities" in 1881. However, the defeat of the communal landholders
did not result in the construction of large export enterprises.

As is well known, only with the growth of the cotton industry after
1945 did large enterprises of that sort appear. Nevertheless, the social
existence of the commercial/landowning "protobourgeoisie" never separated itself from its traditional, lordly, patriarchal roots. That class's
reproduction remained tied to its landowner/commercial condition, a
phenomenon most likely reinforced by the interminable wars between
partisan bands. Those struggles—of many hues and disguises—continued
almost until the very moment of Somoza's flight from Nicaragua in 1979.

Had the Liberal bourgeois coffee growers been able to consolidate
their program, that consolidation would have marked the political demise
of most of the backward forms of class domination and would have
given the state greater power of decision and control. In synthesis, it
would have facilitated the possible establishment of a more national and
bourgeois form of class domination, for that domination would have
been based upon a better integrated society with a single, more unified
dominant class.

Conspiring against that probable outcome were not only internal
difficulties with the emergence of a well-founded agricultural bourgeoisie
but also the conditions imposed by foreign intervention. Indeed, the
bourgeoisie's sensitivity to external power was greater than its deter-

mination to solidify its own internal position. The long-recognized peculiarity of Nicaragua's geostrategic situation tended to bring together— or *excited* might be a better word—those disposed to compromise. At the turn of the century, then, the various elite factions viewed the problem as one of bargaining, of supply in response to foreign demand. Their willingness to entertain various proposals—in effect, to sell the country—made the dominant class's power ever less bourgeois, ever less national.

In order to conclude these brief introductory comments on Nicaragua, I would like to stress two essential aspects. On the one hand, there was the extreme structural heterogeneity of the national economy, marked by the weight of the rural campesino sector and by the relatively self-sufficient character of the large export-oriented estates. That structural heterogeneity posed obstacles to the construction of an integrated domestic market economy conducive to local capital accumulation and therefore impeded the consolidation of the bourgeoisie as a dominant social class.

To be underlined, on the other hand, was the country's dependency vis-à-vis foreign interests, which in Nicaragua's case was not confined merely to those forms of dependency produced through foreign commerce. For beyond those economic bonds lay other forms of dependency originating in foreign centers of power. National elites were extremely sensitive to foreign interests, which in turn, were undoubtedly based on the country's potential to become the site of an interoceanic canal.

National State and Foreign Protectorate

The organization of political power—embodied in the power of the state—always gave the appearance of being a partial power. This was not due so much to its unfinished condition as to an underlying tendency toward its privatization. Battles waged by caudillo leaders, as well as regional rivalries—much like the rest of Central America—transformed the state into the entity from which private interests could best be safeguarded. The economic process required those political privileges, and social groups fought for them intermittently.

The state—constantly in a process of formation and recomposition— received a vigorous "nationalizing impulse" with the Liberal government of Zelaya in the late nineteenth century. The use of the term "impulse" is a reference to the country's preceding lack of territorial unity and to Zelaya's attempts to reestablish sovereign jurisdiction over the entire length and breadth of the country, as well as to the creation of an economic and institutional infrastructure that would facilitate the social integration of the nation.

With the North American military intervention, which began in 1911, the operation and objectives of state power changed directions. Here it is important to recognize that imperialism—as experienced in Nicaragua—was geopolitical rather than economic. It was neither capital investment nor direct control of production within the local market that ultimately justified that military presence. On the contrary, strategic concerns and North American foreign policy were the determining factors. Interference therefore occurred in the state sphere, at the level of political power itself.

Here it makes sense to briefly discuss the role of the state in developing societies. It is well known that the modern state necessarily implies not only societal management by a particular class but also the development of private interests that derive personal benefits through the existence of that state (though acting in name and as representatives of the "nation").

The modern state, then, is the expression and synthesis of a community with a sovereign destiny, marked by a degree of independence that is essential to both its present and its future level of development. And so-called national sovereignty is therefore the autonomous administration of local affairs, the generalization of the relations of domination, of control, and of power within a specific geographical area.

The bourgeois state develops material mechanisms to attain national integration and control as well as to assure the social reproduction of society. It has also been recognized that the more structured those administrative mechanisms are, the more advanced will be the bourgeois foundations of the state. And this is where the state's material apparatus, as well as the public policies that it generates, takes on considerable importance. The preceding, then, is the basic framework that—without many theoretical pretentions—will be used to examine the course of Nicaragua's history leading up to the advent of the Somoza regime.

The occupation by the U.S. Marines must be analyzed in terms of the various levels at which its effects were disruptive. For the occupation was not a foreign invasion in the technical sense of the term, as it was not a subjugating invasion carried out against the national will. It was merely imposed on one defeated, local bourgeois faction by another, with the latter making use of foreign power in order to achieve its own victory.

The success of the Conservative party versus the weak Liberal party bourgeoisie provided the opportunity for North American intervention. That intervention was requested and even applauded by the victorious factions in an intrabourgeois struggle whose true loser was the national state itself.

The first point that should be emphasized here is that the result of hegemony based on military power is not a colony, but rather a political protectorate. In Nicaragua, foreign authority was placed above the authority of the national state, which was still in a formative stage. That foreign authority expropriated and efficiently expedited functions normally reserved for the sphere of so-called public administration. Here it should be remembered that national sovereignty is the capacity both to adopt policy decisions—at the international as well as national level—and to carry them out, via the exercise of state autonomy. The only limitations to that state's policies should be those resulting from the sovereign rights of other national states.

In the case of Nicaragua, however, its protectorate status implied the coexistence of two realms of jurisdiction within the national territory— one of which, because of its subordinate position, yielded final sanction to the other. A substantial contradiction therefore existed in the form of a shared sovereignty, a dually structured decisionmaking process.

What are called in Nicaraguan political history the Dawson Pacts, by which the United States promised loans to Nicaragua in return for control of customs and banking, were something more than a simple achievement of imperialist diplomacy. They were imposed by the U.S. government on October 27, 1910, and accepted by the (self-styled) "victorious" Conservative faction. They constituted the beginning of a juridico-political relationship through which the national state appeared to lose its consistency by turning against the society as a whole. That process was the consequence of carrying out a foreign policy that had clearly negative consequences for that society's general interests. Under those circumstances, the particular interests of the dominant bourgeoisie were also inevitably damaged. Over the course of twenty-three years (1910–1933), Nicaragua was partially governed by a foreign authority and, as a consequence, experienced a situation of shared sovereignty.

Nicaragua was quickly converted into a nation managed by North American bankers taking advantage of their role as creditors. Their activities were supervised by the U.S. State Department and backed by the force of the Marines. The Conservative bourgeoisie's willingness to submit to U.S. tutelage was at least as great as the awareness of inferiority on the part of the entire elite class vis-à-vis North American imperialism.

In the course of those years a strange conjuncture of interests took shape that would long affect the national character of the Nicaraguan commercial-agrarian bourgeoisie. Created during the protectorate, that bourgeoisie gradually became both partner and accomplice in a relationship marked by the dependent status of the national state—a relationship approaching that of a colony to its colonizer.

In its classical version, imperialism constitutes an internal economic presence within a dependent society. Dependency is precisely that articulation of forces in which foreign interests appear to define themselves as a domestic factor at the economic and political level. Foreign capital investments and their capture of a share of the domestic market promote a certain degree of development of local productive forces as well as determining brief periods of economic growth. On occasion they also encourage tendencies more oriented toward diversification and the relative modernization of the economic apparatus.

However, the North American presence in Nicaragua was of another sort. Discounting investments in the mining of precious metals—which were genuine neocolonial enclaves—U.S. interests were geopolitical. The canal concession, signed by one of the "historic" caudillo leaders of the Conservative faction, Emiliano Chamorro, constitutes the principal element within that constellation of strategic interests.

The task that concerns us here is that of determining the degree to which this peculiar form of foreign control either damaged or assisted the development of a local bourgeoisie, of a dominant class, and of a national state. In relation to that process, imperialism acted in a profoundly contradictory manner. To illustrate this point one need only recall the intentions made explicit over that long period by the Dawson Pacts, by the loans from Brown Brothers Bank, by the monetary law and monetary reform, and by the creation of the central bank. But even more important were the actions of the High Commission, the financial plans of 1917 and 1920, and the figure of the tax collector general—of U.S. nationality— who acted de facto as a superminister of the Treasury.

In addition, there was the role assumed by the High Commission— composed of *one* Nicaraguan and *two* North Americans—placed under the supervision of the State Department. Finally, of course, came the tasks of public order, control, and repression at the hands of the Marine Infantry Corps, which in fact undertook the role of a national police force.

The military occupation of Nicaragua—as well as the control of various key economic and political institutions at the national level— resulted in an extended delay in the construction of the national state's capacity for the autonomous administration of local affairs. Given that a truly national bourgeoisie is by definition a governing bourgeoisie— and vice versa—sharing hegemony was tantamount to losing it. But at the same time, the protectorate status allowed U.S. imperialism to create or modernize several spheres of control—customs, the armed forces, and an initial system of taxation—which would later be used to sustain local forms of domination.

In any event, the national character of the state obviously suffered to the degree that its policies were subordinated to a superior, foreign power. That subordination in turn lessened the leadership potential of the bourgeois class as a whole, though the damage was hardly perceived at the time.

U.S. intervention, in the final analysis, favored the constitution of the material apparatus of domination in its repressive, controlling dimension. The Constabulary—as the National Guard was originally called—was created as a police corps composed of officers who were to be entrusted with the maintenance of public order. It mirrored the image of other forces created by the North Americans—with uneven success—in the Philippines, Haiti, and the Dominican Republic.

The "Somocista" State:
Dynastic, Hereditary, and Plebeian Power

At the time of the intervention, the Nicaraguan bourgeoisie existed only in an incipient form, created through its activities in commerce and agriculture (coffee, cattle, sugar). The bourgeoisie lived largely closed off from the rest of society, within the small world of the hacienda or of local intercity rivalries.

Apparently, the economic interests of the rural caudillo leaders were not directly affected by the intervention. To the contrary, the foreign presence facilitated a more efficient organization of the domestic economy and may, therefore, have actually stimulated the mercantile sector.

However, members of the bourgeoisie wound up exercising direct control of power, and it was through the rigors of the political game that their governing qualities matured. Moreover, the unification of the bourgeoisie as a class took place within the confines of the state, and that class's dominant character emanated from state constitutions.

It is within that framework of these domestic and foreign parameters that Anastasio Somoza García, director-in-chief of the National Guard, entered the scene as representative, receiver, and wielder of power on January 10, 1933. And given that historical background, it is not mere rhetoric to assert that Somoza was the direct descendant of U.S. intervention and of the pacification of Nicaragua's Segovia Mountains.

But Somoza was also the eminent product of a backward agricultural society. That backwardness produced and nurtured the class struggles that accompanied the entire lengthy period of foreign military occupation (1911–1933), as well as those that followed, intermittently, in later years. That general context of continuing struggle helps explain the domineering, personalized nature (*caudillaje y personalismo*) of Nicaraguan political life.

Throughout the entire occupation period, the class struggle remained masked as a political tussle between the dominant agricultural-commercial factions. That struggle itself was indicative of the society's backwardness. Bickering between small, rival elite factions—which for generations had produced firm, traditional loyalties to either the Liberal or Conservative party—only remotely resembled the defense of class interests.

Indeed, the traditional political groupings did not correspond to sector-based class factions. They were much more the consequence of political frictions that stimulated old family loyalties or caudillo rivalries. Those struggles and their repercussions did not favor the bourgeoisie's fundamental strategic end: the diffusion and consolidation of capitalism through the establishment of capitalist agricultural enterprises based on the exploitation of free wage labor.

Those confrontations adopted a peculiar hue because of the North American occupation, which had become an important—if not determinant—element of political power, and which unleashed new kinds of rivalry. The battles only reinforced the enduring quislinglike (*entreguista*) behavior of submissive Liberal-Conservative factions.

However, a sense of national shame eventually produced the first popular struggles against the invader. Though initially rather elementary, those popular struggles in any case represented a violent rejection of the physical and political brutality of the North American intervention as well as of the servility of the two traditional parties. It was that same anti-imperialist consciousness that the FSLN later recognized and revived.

Here it is important to recall the struggle and heroic sacrifice of Benjamín Zeledón and the Liberal army, who confronted North American troops in Masaya in 1911. Also noteworthy was the attitude of the National Assembly, which in 1911 approved and sustained the constitution, rejecting the rude impositions of the North Americans made through Chamorro and his group. In ensuing years there was also resistance on the part of various Liberal leaders.

All of those nationalist actors and events helped prepare the way for Sandino's refusal to sign the Pact of Espino Negro in the town of Tipitapa and for his subsequent decision to rise up in a popular insurrection against foreign occupation, in 1927. Thus Sandino himself was the product of a long gestation process, which took place in the very heart of Nicaraguan society in order to confront the invader. In the same way, the FSLN was the national, confrontational response to the dictatorship inherited from that invader.

Recounting the Somozas' personal intrigues is of no great interest here, for their combined biography is little more than a sordid tale. Worthwhile, however, is a brief summary of what those intrigues reveal.

The character of Somoza García, for example, was only confirmed by the manner in which he climbed the ladder to power. That path was indicative of a number of his principal personality traits, among them opportunism, corruption, and amorality. However, the key aspect of his character was not its absolute lack of scruples, but rather the kind of conscience that generally accompanies such deficiencies.

Those personal intrigues also help explain the social roots underlying personal dictatorship in that backward society, whose bourgeois cycle had just begun. The Somozas' behavior was "caudillo-like," tending toward the privatization of public power.

The Somoza era began February 21, 1934, with the assassination of Sandino and the merciless pacification of the Segovias. It ended July 17, 1979, with the dictator's flight to Miami, a city apparently destined to become, among other things, the social garbage dump of capitalist history. It was a period of forty-five years—almost a half-century— during which oligarchical domination was both prolonged and changed. Nonetheless, following the formal end of the intervention in 1933, that oligarchy was never quite able to adapt to the new situation.

It is difficult and probably unnecessary to examine the oligarchical nature of class domination under the conditions created by U.S. intervention. The oligarchic presence—understood as the social predominance of agricultural and commercial interests—was only reduced in the strictest sense: Its culture and emotional evolution occurred with constant reference to the United States.

Throughout the period of the intervention, the leading figures and institutions of economic and political life deferred their key decisions to the guiding existence of a superior foreign force. Beneath the shelter provided by that guiding force—which did have limits to the extent that it represented political and cultural power—both economic growth and political struggles were able to continue. In other words, the bourgeoisie and the bourgeois state evolved in the shadow of imperialism.

We have spoken of the "Somocista" state only in order to make use of that adjective as a provisional qualifier. The state formed by the Somoza regime does not in itself constitute a "model" of the state in the classical sense, as it does not correspond to a distinct, specific phase in the development of capitalist modes of production. The Somocista state was but one feasible form of government—expressing one possible manner of exercising power—given the particular structure and articulation of Nicaraguan political institutions. Over the course of that near half-century, the social organization of production changed, as did the structure of the laboring classes and their position vis-à-vis political power. But the all-powerful dictatorial figure—the caudillo, the chief (*jefe*), the president—was maintained without alterations.

At the base of Nicaragua's profound political crisis, which began in late 1972, was the imbalance underlying relationships between various social sectors. Moreover, that crisis could not be resolved by an internal redefinition of power, as the dictatorial regime had undoubtedly exhausted all possible options for prolonging its hegemony.

Here the inevitably tragic limits of personal power are implicit. The social imbalance alludes to the relative deepening of capitalist relations and forms of production. In the Nicaraguan case, the latter developed extremely rapidly; first in the export agricultural sector and later via the emergence of a concentrated industrial nucleus. But while this was occurring neither the state apparatus nor its class expression adjusted to the changes.

The Somocista state combined both general characteristics typical of a backward configuration of class power and particular characteristics resulting from the specificities of Nicaraguan society. In the latter sense, that state was first and foremost a form of power that not only originated in foreign intervention but that was also built up and given validity by that intervention. It was constructed from the very beginning as a personal form of power, the project of a military caudillo for whom the electoral process only served to ratify the victory achieved through other means.

In its oligarchic definition, the exclusion of the subordinate classes was not a matter of force but rather an aspect of society so obvious and natural that it was elementary. The power game was a battle of competing interests and influence among prominent members of society, among members of an aristocratic family whose position had been secured via the extraordinary force of tradition and wealth.

In effect, the crisis of the traditional parties and oligarchic forms of political representation occurred within the Somoza regime. But it was a slowly developing crisis, involving the dissolution and reconstitution of the party's governing style, much as if it had been a political soiree of the elite.

A change of title—for example, from chief of state to secretary general—was something more than a mere terminological substitution. It implied a partial break with the hereditary tradition and with personalized loyalties, which for more than a century made the war between Liberals and Conservatives a battle between campesinos commanded by land-owners.

The Conservative party, the older and more closed of the two, has remained excluded from the exercise of governmental responsibilities since the end of the Constitutionalist War in 1927. It never again gained control of political power, though shares of power were obtained on two occasions via deals made between one of the party's factions and the incumbent dictator: Somoza García in 1952 and Anastasio Somoza Debayle in 1970. In any case, these pacts were not business deals between equals, but rather shady complicities from which the dictatorship always emerged victorious.

The old Liberal party was also unable to maintain its unity and its political importance. One faction—certainly a majority—supported Somoza García's coup d'état against President Juan B. Sacasa (the uncle of Somoza's wife) and stayed by his side during the ensuing elections as well as throughout his term as constitutional president, from 1937 to 1943. That faction formed the Party of National Liberation (PLN). Meanwhile another Liberal faction, the Independent Liberal party (PLI), remained steadfastly in the opposition.

The state of mind that divided the social structure vertically between Liberals and Conservatives—at times relying on little more than the hatred marking family feuds—was discarded for the first time with Sandino's military alignment and was later resumed with the creation of the FSLN. Both movements constituted important elements within the crisis of the traditional parties, whereas the FSLN represented the conspicuous expression of that crisis's resolution.

In order to better characterize the Somocista regime—as well as the Nicaraguan state that functioned throughout that long contemporary period—it will be necessary to present several analytical synopses corresponding to the stages of that history. For example, in order to understand the role of the state within the dictatorial regime, it is necessary to focus specifically on the consolidation of that regime. In this first stage—as in that of its further development during the second generation of Somozas—the complicity of North American imperialism was quite evident and remained a constant element of the dictatorship until its fall in July 1979. Also apparent was the repeated collaboration of various bourgeois factions, as they too consolidated their social positions. The following is a review of those stages.

1. The consolidation of the dictatorial structure was produced primarily via the effects of two critical moments. On the one hand, there were the effects of the global capitalist crisis of 1930, which had long-term repercussions in Nicaragua, disorganizing economic life and leading to further profoundly destructive consequences in terms of debilitated productive forces. On the other hand, there was Sandino's war of liberation, which lasted from 1927 to 1933. Nicaraguan society remained stagnant during that period, and it was only toward the early 1940s that demand for war products—rubber, wood, essential oils—and an increase in the volume of exportable coffee began to reactivate the long-paralyzed economy.

That period coincides with the stage of the consolidation of authoritarian military regimes—supported by the United States—in Central America and the Caribbean, as an appropriate means of stabilizing the region. The first Somoza period was stable largely because it formed a part of that continental strategy.

Obviously, the dictatorship was not merely a product of foreign will and influence. They merely represented the necessary conditions permitting internal factors to operate fully. The sufficient conditions included the political tradition of the country; its backward economy and culture; the presence of a coherent and modernized institution like the National Guard; the complicity of a large part of the oligarchy; and of course, Somoza's personal appetites. Thus the structure of authoritarian power, whose roots extended well back into the nation's history, found a fertilizer capable of invigorating those roots amid the disastrous climate of the depression years.

In the situation of profound social disorganization that followed the withdrawal of the U.S. Marines, Nicaraguan society entered a relatively calm period. It has been interpreted as a brief stage of intraclass reconciliation, though that peace was undoubtedly more proclaimed than real.

Vengeance had been a historic trait of the Conservative party, and that attitude would normally have been expected to continue after the Liberal party's ascent to power under Somoza. But in truth, the liquidation of Sandino and the elimination of the threat of his campesino rebel army received the approval of all the large landowners. In effect, the pacification of the Segovias served not only as a tranquilizing expedient for perturbed oligarchic minds, but also as a successful extraeconomic means of ridding formerly occupied zones of those campesinos who had fought with Sandino's army. As such, the defeat of Sandinismo was hardly a liberal defeat.

The way in which Somoza achieved access to executive power was precisely what enabled his later consolidation as the indispensable national "caudillo." Here it is worthwhile mentioning some of the background to that ascent. Repeating a formula used several years before, the 1936 elections offered a combined Liberal-Conservative civilian candidacy. Meanwhile Washington, which, by virtue of the Central American accords of 1907 and 1923, had been applying a policy of nonrecognition of non–de jure governments, broke with that regional foreign policy when it recognized the blood-stained de facto government of Maximiliano Hernández Martínez in 1936.

Somoza organized the coup d'état against Sacasa in June 1936. All the while, he maintained an impeccable attention to the requirements of the constitution. For example, he had the congress elect his good friend Carlos Brenes Jarquín interim president, then forced him to call new elections six months after Sacasa had abandoned the government in order to comply with minimum stipulations regarding the presidential succession of relatives.

Soon thereafter, Somoza stepped down from his post as director-in-chief of the National Guard, where he was replaced by Colonel Rigoberto Reyes. After having himself nominated as Liberal party presidential candidate—as well as that of a faction of the Conservative party—he managed to garner 107,000 votes in his favor, with only 169 votes for the opposition, in the elections of 1937. Somoza thereby emerged with total power and a legitimate government, in addition to being the country's "peacemaker."

2. With the dictatorial machinery assembled upon foundations set in the power of the National Guard, what occurred thereafter was nothing more than an almost inevitable corollary. Here the common tendency toward the concentration of political power had immediate effects, as well as exceptional causes.

While the combined effects of Sandino's war of liberation and those of the crisis of the 1930s help to explain the early support enjoyed by the General of the Virgin Sword,[1] the political consequences of World War II also served to promote the prolongation of that predominance into a second term.

At the same time, North American policy favored the electoral victories of the region's dictators during that period: of General Ubico in 1937 and 1943 in Guatemala; of Hernández Martínez in the same years in El Salvador; and those of Carías Andino, in Honduras, in 1936 and 1942. Internal stability in the North American "backyard" was more important than even the legality of international treaties that—as in the treaty of 1923—forbade the recognition of any Central American government coming to power by nonconstitutional means.

This second stage in the history of the Somoza dictatorship included the first and second reelections of Somoza García (1940, 1951) and ended with his death September 21, 1956, shortly after his nomination for a fourth term by the Liberal party. Both the limitations and potential of centralized, authoritarian, and personalized structures of power appear in this period. The course pursued by the elder Somoza's heirs was nothing more than the extension to their limits of characteristics inherent to an atrocious form of class domination.

With the end of World War II, Somoza's economic roots became further consolidated. In accordance with the agricultural nature of the diverse factions of the Nicaraguan oligarchy, Somoza placed himself in their very center as that class's most important figure.[2] In his time he was the most important cattle dealer in Nicaragua and rivaled the traditional large coffee growers of León and Grenada for the top spot in that sector.

From the very beginning the dictator enjoyed competitive advantages in the market through the systematic manipulation of both the exercise of power and the administration of public affairs. He then exploited that political power as a useful complement to his private properties. Some analysts have viewed this phenomenon as an expression of patrimonial power, which must be explained within the context of a precapitalist society. We will return to this point a bit further on.

There is another important characteristic that together with the former—and also encountered within the semiautonomous "political sphere"—completes the character of the Nicaraguan state. That characteristic concerns the traditional Conservative oligarchy, whose roles both as class and as political subject were not eliminated. Neither the tardy expansion of agricultural capitalism nor the exclusion of members of that oligarchy from the government after 1927 was able to defeat them.

Though they lost the personal favors and sympathy of U.S. officials in charge of relations with Nicaragua, their role in the political game continued. There was always a Conservative party group in the opposition, just as there was always another group ready to make deals and to seek resolution—through negotiation—of the issues that divided them. At the most critical junctures, as the elder Somoza liked to say, it was necessary to reach an agreement with the Conservatives.

The political regime was characterized, then, by its special bipartisan features. The preeminence of the Liberal party was tied to its evolution into an official party resembling a bureaucratic extension of the state itself. Normal political party roles—such as constituency representation, the channeling of interests, legitimation by either real or implied consensus, and so on—were always of lesser importance.

In the intraoligarchic struggle as well as the inevitable divisions among the local bourgeoisie, the traditional parties were always the key players in the political game. It is discouraging—if not impossible—to follow the trail of domestic rifts, recompositions, alliances, and betrayals that interwove Nicaraguan political life under the Somozas.

One only entered the legal, public game of politics wearing either a Liberal or Conservative party mask. The rules of that game revolved therefore around a bipartisan elite, whose chances of participating directly in the government differed according to party affiliation, despite shared upper-class origins. Therefore neither a Social-Christian nor a Social-Democratic party ever prospered, much less those of a Marxist tendency. Again, it was the FSLN that managed to escape the political straitjacket, disqualifying the entire lot of quarrelsome bourgeois factions as accomplices of equally low stature. In fact, the Conservative bourgeoisie served successively as enemy and partner of the Liberal bourgeoisie in a struggle that eventually dragged down the other classes as well.

The democratizing wave arising from the fervor of the antifascist victory, a wave that adopted a clearly antioligarchic position throughout Central America, also swept through Nicaragua. At this point it is worthwhile recalling that between 1944 and 1948 all of the governments arising from the crisis of the 1930s—regimes whose viability was extended during World War II via imperialist support—were replaced violently. In Nicaragua, the first major anti-Somoza mass movement developed in 1944, led by the Conservative Youth.[3]

In any case, the rules of the conflict had been altered. Elsewhere—in Guatemala, El Salvador, and Costa Rica—new social forces emerged on the political stage. Their common denominator (beyond their shared class origins as professionals, lower and middle bourgeoisie, and so on) was the pursuit of new and different options within the general framework of a limited bourgeois democracy. But in Nicaragua it was the Conservatives—possessing scant antioligarchic zeal—who founded the democratic struggles, via their campaigns against Somoza. Those efforts, however, ended in failure. As both a consequence and a corollary of that regional wave, the reelection of Somoza was postponed. His Liberal party was forced to approve the candidacy of an old rival, Leonardo Argüello, for the elections of February 1947.

It is worthwhile examining this episode in some detail because it constituted a test for the personalized, kingly, and antidemocratic nature of Somocista power. Indeed Argüello was elected, defeating a coalition of Conservatives and Liberals. Somoza retained control of the National Guard and two months later called on its support in order to overthrow the elderly, stubborn President Argüello. Somoza then had his uncle Benjamín Lacayo Sacasa nominated as successor. That government lasted all of twenty-two days. It was at this point that a special convocation of the Constituent Assembly chose yet another uncle, Víctor Román y Reyes, to don the presidential sash.

An aspect that deserves attention in the course of those events is the dictator's apparent scrupulous concern for the maintenance of legal forms in order to secure his reelection, much like the maneuvers he had used preceding his first election. This time he had to wait until 1951 and even then had to make a deal with the Conservatives. Political ethics—completely absent during the period—can hardly explain that essentially opportunistic strategy. But part of the explanation lies with the United States, whose diplomats convinced Somoza García to follow those steps. The Pact of the Generals between Emilio Chamorro and Anastasio Somoza Debayle in 1959 would repeat the formula that had been tried in the town of Cuadra Pasos years before. It was to be the same search for a modus vivendi with the Conservative faction of the bourgeoisie, who were always disposed to negotiate, or—in more direct language—to barter the price of their cooperation.

By virtue of the 1950 pact, the Conservative party received minority participation in the central government and in autonomous institutions, as well as a smaller slice—one-third—of the seats in parliament. It should also be remembered that the accompanying authorization for Somoza's fourth term as dictator was based largely within a climate produced by a period of the most rapid economic growth in the history of Nicaragua.

The unruly faction of the agrarian bourgeoisie, with its bastions in the Conservative party, received political guarantees in return for its collaboration. Those guarantees assured the members of this faction that the recently opened process of capital accumulation—which benefited them directly—would be maintained without competition or deception.

3. The third stage of the consolidation and crisis of the Somocista state corresponds to the period in which the dictator's descendants inherited power and carried the previously mentioned characteristics of his regime to its ultimate consequences. Within that process of power concentration there was confusion from above concerning spheres of competition and from below concerning the distinction between the public and the private and in the realm of personal business dealings. Beyond that, of course, there was also repression and corruption. The third stage covers a period of twenty-four more years, which began September 21, 1956, with the death of Somoza García at the hands of the heroic Nicaraguan poet Rigoberto López Pérez. On the very day of his death, Somoza was preparing for his fifth presidential term.

Once again the details of how republican formalities were altered to the advantage of dynastic predilections only serve to ratify the arrogant nature of the family's power. Twenty-four hours after the death of his father, the congress entrusted Luis Somoza Debayle with the completion of the presidential term, based upon his position as president of the Chamber of Deputies.[4] Luis, in turn, immediately nominated his brother, Anastasio Somoza Debayle, as director-in-chief of the National Guard.[5]

According to a general definition, dynastic structures are those family formations whose individual members successfully perpetuate the family's power. This conceptualization helps to focus the analysis on how that continuity was achieved in a society such as Nicaragua's, which had already begun to change.

The Somoza García period—above all during its initial stage—clearly moved within the framework of a backward socioeconomic structure in crisis, in which a military caudillo and oligarchic behavior were able to take advantage of the corresponding weakly developed political system.

In any case, the presence of the National Guard—a small, relatively modern, professional army that was also extremely dependent on foreign support—became a separate factor in the equation of political power. It also altered previous conditions affecting the existence and development of the oligarchic factor, which had long been a particular form of class domination, of political/ideological culture, and of power originating directly from the rural social origins of its leaders.

The elder Somoza—whose class interests at the end of his life were those of a cattleman and coffee grower—was without doubt a typical Latin American dictator of the oligarchic era. However, his reign was an exceptional one to the extent that he grew stronger after 1940, when the decline of his Latin American counterparts was already obvious. In Nicaragua, the crisis of oligarchic domination was dissolved in a process of another nature. It is also important to add that the state that corresponded to that dictatorship was never really consolidated in a manner similar to that which occurred—though in varying fashion—in Costa Rica, Guatemala, and El Salvador.

During the "constitutionalist" period of Somoza I coffee prices increased, and by 1946 they reached a level seven times higher than their previous low. According to Jaime Wheelock,[6] the Law of Land Surveying, which had been suspended, was reactivated in 1950, with predictable results: the sale and expropriation of uncultivated lands together with the violent expropriation of campesino properties. That process not only pushed back the commercial agricultural frontier but also altered the landscape of traditional farming in the humid Pacific coastlands of Nicaragua.

However, cotton rather than coffee was the product that most favored capitalism's great advance throughout the country. The ephemeral but vigorous triumph of export agriculture brought with it the slow and incomplete consolidation of a bourgeoisie that never lived up to its class calling, due to the political cycle within which that economic growth took place. The cotton boom stimulated the agricultural capitalist cycle and brought it to unprecedented levels. In the lapse of twelve years, 80 percent of cultivable land on the Pacific Coast was converted to cotton cultivation (175,000 hectares), with an annual growth rate of 18 percent over the first six years.

Between 1950 and 1972 (the year of the earthquake) the value of coffee exports rose from $17.3 to $32.9 million, while cotton increased dramatically from $1.8 to $62.2 million.[7] Cattle and sugarcane also emerged during that period as products that substantially transformed the national economic order.

The evolution of the Nicaraguan economy entered a stage of vigorous expansion—first with the modernization of export agriculture and later with the industrializing opportunities of the Central American Common Market. That economic expansion had distinct repercussions in the political sphere, where maintenance of the plebeian Somoza dynasty was achieved.

In February 1957 Luis Somoza was elected with that kind of suspect majority that all well-executed frauds require. As usual, there was a Conservative candidate—this time, Edmundo Amador—in order to re-establish the foundations of simulated democracy.

In 1963, due to profound internal discord as well as to North American opposition, the Nationalist Liberal party was compelled to propose a civilian candidate—René Schick, a former employee of Somoza—who lived up to expectations by defeating his rival by a ratio of ten votes to one. This time, the losing conservative candidate was Diego Manuel Chamorro.

During the period of interregnum between the two Anastasios, the hereditary nature of the family's power was not altered. Luis Somoza retained leadership of the party and Anastasio Junior that of the National Guard.

But even before the premature death of Schick, party machinery had been moving toward the ratification of what was already evident in the course of the country's political affairs; that is, the candidacy of Anastasio Junior, or Somoza III.

The months prior to the elections of February 5, 1967, reveal the increasingly unruly and bourgeois character of the Conservative opposition. Those primaries will not go down as the most fraudulent in liberal history, perhaps because of the difficulty of measuring the exact dimensions of an electoral sham. However, having faced a formidable civic opposition on the verge of popular insurrection, and having employed repressive mechanisms in order to assure the victory of Somoza III, the beginnings of a slow but inevitable decline of the dictatorial structure became manifest. By that time, the FSLN had already been formed, and its path clearly marked by a string of initial defeats.

The Revolutionary Crisis of the State

Throughout the entire period being examined in this chapter there are two sets of phenomena worth analyzing. Both are inevitably variables of any model of dictatorial power, and their longevity in Nicaraguan history converted them into features of the state's very survival. One of those features—and the most generic—was the impossibility of establishing legitimate forms of political power that would, at the same time, be legal. Liberal theory accepted that dichotomy, thereby justifying the use of so-called emergency laws, which sought to resolve the latter of those requisites.

The preceding distinction between legality and legitimacy alludes to the nature of a dictatorial form of power that survived via the minimum fulfillment of the formalities of the liberal democratic order. That distinction, in any case, eventually leads to the discussion of an even greater problem: Can a system of political domination base itself upon structural foundations that cannot be legitimated over the passage of time?

Dictatorship is by definition illegitimate, but beginning at least with Hellenic tradition, it could nonetheless be considered legal. In those classical cases, dictatorship was justified as an exceptional state of affairs required in the face of abnormal circumstances. It survived in the form of a transitory discrepancy, to be replaced via normal mechanisms of readaptation and adjustment. We also know that totalitarian fascist dictatorships created their own legality within a normative system answering only to itself. The legality of the state is therefore a tautological affair, since by definition its existence will always be legal in the sense that the state is based upon a self-justifying constitutive will.

However, within bourgeois tradition the state can also be illegitimate. Here it is important to look at the relationship between state and class. The problem of legitimacy revolves around the class interests of the dominant bourgeoisie. It is inconceivable that a bourgeois form of power, enjoying its role as manager of general societal affairs, would place the state in a position detrimental to the particular interests of that same dominant class.

The problem of the legal foundations of the Somoza state was resolved throughout its nearly half-century of existence via repeated violation and recomposition of political norms. On March 22, 1937—shortly after the first election of Somoza I—a Constituent Assembly marked by futility revoked the 1911 constitution. The purpose behind that move was to avoid the elections set for 1940 (presidential terms were then four years)—in which Somoza would not have been allowed to participate—and to constitutionally elect him for the 1940–1946 period. In effect, by evading the elections of 1941, Somoza García held on to power illegally for ten years.

On April 15, 1948, a new constitution was passed in order to authorize another reelection. Ten years later, in April 1958, the constitution was reformed again—this time with Conservative votes—in order to avoid Luis Somoza's reelection. Those reforms granted women's suffrage and reduced the presidential term to four years but—more importantly—left the door open for the election of Anastasio Junior. And in May 1962, various articles of the constitution were revised once again.

Finally, in 1972, by virtue of the final deal between the traditional parties—known as the Agüero-Somoza Pact—the Constituent Assembly modified the books in order to confirm a certain degree of Conservative party participation and to authorize Somoza Debayle's hold on government until 1980.

Legitimacy was sought within the deep bipartisan tradition that ran through the entire history of the Somoza regime and marked its crises. That is, pacts were often sought—and always violated—with the Conservative party.

However, the passing from one generation to another also entailed changes in the society. As such, the oligarchical period ended in confusion with Somoza "the landowner," while the military-bureaucratic style strengthened itself during the era of Somoza "the transnational." The latter process presaged the enormous difficulties that would face the bourgeoisie in its efforts to reconstruct the old system of alliances—a system managed much better by the elder Somoza than by his son.

The other set of aforementioned phenomena that were constant in the workings of the Nicaraguan dictatorial structure involved the confusion—more real than apparent—between public, national affairs of the community and the private interests of the family, individuals, small firms, and corporations.

The contradiction was resolved in the very moment of Somoza García's ascent to power via the application of a perverse Central American tradition: To the victor go the spoils! That prepolitical custom was a relic of the nineteenth-century wars between oligarchic factions. Under the Somozas it led to a brutal and insatiable accumulation: first of wealth, and then of capital. That accumulation process transformed the Somoza family, without any doubt, into the number one business group in Central America. Certainly forty-odd years are plenty of time to build a solid capital base, from one generation to the next. What demands attention here is the fact that this accumulation could only have been achieved via the utilization of the entire state apparatus responsible for public policy and the management of international aid, as well as through the most vicious exploitation of Nicaraguan workers.

Tactics included influence peddling and a mixture of both open and veiled bribery—standard mechanisms used by bourgeoisies everywhere. The control of power created a multiplicity of conditions not only for those activities but also for the use of strategic investment opportunities, for fly-by-night businesses, for high-risk bank loans, and for the thousand-and-one forms that administrative corruption can assume today. The concentrated and authoritarian structure of the Somozas' personalized power facilitated that process even more. The state, therefore—though not the location where capital creation and accumulation took place—was indeed the entity whose concurrence made that process possible.

The dictatorship developed capitalism in Nicaragua in highly concentrated fashion, with bourgeois benefits falling primarily to the Somoza family itself but also extending to a circle of friends and servants closely tied to that family. At the story's close in 1979, there were some twenty generals whose average wealth was an estimated $18 million.

The Somocista circle consisted of a vast conglomerate of various enterprises. The mechanisms of the enrichment process resemble—though only formally—those procedures that the grand vizier placed at the disposition of his close circle of favorites in order to assure their prosperity. Because those procedures were accompanied by a high level of physical violence and arbitrariness—while always being perceived as personal concessions from the caliph—they produced a structure of loyalties with striking similarities to the patrimonial game of feudal domination.[8]

In that particular context, public administration was managed by a government of strictly private affairs. And for that reason, the common impression that emerged—from almost any perspective—was that of a nation governed within a regal vision of power: One who leads does so by divine right, according to personal whim.

The decisive element of the dictatorial situation was the further consolidation of an important local bourgeoisie—concomitant with the surge of the Somocistas—which continued to grow within the traditional parameters of the preceding system. While financing the propagation of their dominant ideology, the wealth of coffee growers, cattle farmers, and merchants was also converted into industrial and financial capital. Two concurring factors of internal origin made that conversion possible: the demand for cotton and foreign capital investments in Central American Common Market industries.

The export of cotton—which played such an important role in the renovation of the traditional social order in Nicaragua—also had political consequences. Here it is worthwhile pointing out that cotton is an annual crop whose production can be altered from year to year in response to forecasts of international demand and prices and therefore constitutes a typical business venture of a highly speculative nature. The crop also required a new type of producer: modern, management oriented, and capable of gathering together preexisting productive factors at any given moment. For that reason, its implantation and development could not be achieved outside the state realm, nor without its protection.

In short, cotton developed in Central America as a political export fiber. The boom in Nicaragua required access to credit, legal mechanisms, and the recourse to force, all of which were put at the disposal of opportunistic bourgeois entrepreneurs. Those entrepreneurs were always attentive to signs of market change and attuned to the distinctive chords of political concessions. A robust and durable bourgeoisie was unable to establish itself as a consequence of the cotton boom. Rather, a particular form of venture capital—itinerant and highly concentrated—contributed in large part to the formation of Nicaraguan financial capital.

The other important factor was the investment by transnational companies—and foreign capital in general—in manufacturing industries. That investment carried with it a variety of operational forms: the displacement of local businesses; association with local companies in order to facilitate their rapid modernization; and the direct implantation of new foreign-owned firms. Although Nicaragua did not particularly benefit from the regional integration project in its early years, by the 1970s significant rates of growth in production had been achieved.

Growth and consolidation of more advanced bourgeois sectors took place in the 1950s, when large business groups were formed around private interests that apparently corresponded to those of the old Conservative and Liberal oligarchy. Some became associated with the Bank of America group (Banamérica), founded in 1952, and some with the Bank of Nicaragua (Banic), formed in 1953.

It is rather useless to attempt a description of those groups, which have proven difficult to define precisely. Nevertheless, they were essentially elite financial associations that connected the most diverse of business interests at various levels. Their financial capital was linked to large North American financial corporations and they undertook a variety of intricate and mysterious business dealings with the Somoza Group. And that which has been united by the market let not politics tear asunder.

The last point that ought to be examined is the fact that in its final phase of evolution, the Somocista state was unable to establish itself as a modern bourgeois state. The economy—though hardly an autonomous sphere—was increasingly capitalist, as was most clearly the Somoza Group itself.

However, backwardness at the political-ideological level was apparent. The exercise of state power was conducted in an extremely direct manner, that is, without the presence of independent, intermediary bodies. That power was not only transformed into a dictatorship—with all of the traditional features—but also became personalized.

At the same time, the state refused to tolerate typical bourgeois means of societal control, such as parliamentary representation, judicial jurisdiction, a system of free elections including the political party game, and the organization of trade unions. An excessively centralized state system was then established, forming an almost total and absolute power—de facto—in the face of which all existing competition disappeared. The figure of the president of the republic emerged and became confused with that of the director-in-chief of the National Guard as well as that of the party leader.

Here it should be noted that this "seizure of jurisdictions" did not correspond in any way to the control of jurisdictions characteristic of a bourgeois state nor to the common methods of bourgeois class domination. Indeed, though its powers may appear to have been unlimited, the Somocista state never implied the elimination or dissolution of the constitutional-juridical framework. Those institutional takeovers were—as political theory might define them—seizures corresponding to de facto legal proceedings.

The functioning of the state under such conditions takes on an exceptional character. The Nicaraguan state at the end of the Somoza era was not "the state of all the people," nor did it represent the nation. It operated under conditions that established a distance between state and society mediated via open repression by the National Guard on the one hand and by the Liberal party—as a bureaucratic instrument of recruitment and ideological control—on the other.

In reality, social life was marked by a minimum rule of law and civil rights (which explains that state's character, despite its toleration of an opposition newspaper like *La Prensa* and the existence of an opposing political party such as that of the Conservatives). The typical informality of Nicaraguan political culture continued, paralleled by the free rein enjoyed by the authoritarian core in relation to the wide gamut of its activities. In that way, power did not only become more centralized. For to the extent that authority was maximized, arbitrariness also grew.

Actually, it is not correct to speak merely of personal power, nor would it be appropriate to discuss that power solely in terms of the Somoza family. No matter how backward Nicaraguan society may have been, it would have been impossible to govern the country through a single individual, the dictator. The personalization of power is something else again and corresponds to a prebourgeois expression of political control that brings us closer to the Weberian definition of traditional domination.

The Somoza dynasty could only retain power because it was capable of building an administrative framework that provided extraordinarily effective support. The key elements of that framework were the *army* and the *party;* that is to say, a combination of terror and corruption. The two groups served to distribute punishments and favors—of ever-changing dimensions and quality—over the forty years of the Somoza regime.

That entire construct of power—whose visible head was Somoza—was a fundamentally weak state apparatus. Its weakness became only more apparent as the political crisis devoured all but the apparatus's head and bones. The state's fragility was further revealed through successive events that marked that crisis: the earthquake of December 1972; the successful hostage taking of December 1975, and of course the assassination of Pedro Joaquín Chamorro in January 1978.

A strong state is a state enjoying social support and consensus, where "civil society" maintains and reproduces the "internalized acceptance of institutions and laws."[9] But a state that substitutes brute force for class hegemony is nothing more than an armed state—difficult to destroy, but vulnerable nonetheless. This dialectical contradiction between the strength of arms and the weakness of bourgeois power was extremely advantageous to the Nicaraguan people in their struggle against the dictatorship and was a particularly effective element in the FSLN's strategy during the final months of the insurrection.

Somoza Debayle revealed a limited bourgeois awareness through the way in which he managed alliances. He did not seek deals with potential allies, deals that had become necessary in order to save the class as a whole. And here it should be remembered that not only the common people, but also an important sector of the Nicaraguan bourgeoisie, opposed the dictatorship.

Somoza's resistance resembled that of a traditional landowner, thereby creating conditions that fed the popular insurrection. What had been military power became political weakness, and the triumph of the Sandinista offensive therefore meant the defeat of both imperialism and the local bourgeoisie. The collapse of the backward political-ideological superstructure carried with it the bourgeois base of society. After twenty-two years of U.S. intervention and forty-four years of Somocismo, the nation finally recovered its identity July 17, 1979, via the destruction of that state that had oppressed it for so long.

As has been said on other occasions, this is not the moment to apply labels or headings. To the degree that socialism is not an act of faith, but rather a decision taken upon the terrain of politics and the state— and within limits established by the economy—an analysis of that transition will be postponed to a later date. It is the Nicaraguan people's turn to speak.

Notes

1. Anastasio Somoza García was promoted to the rank of general within a typical framework of backward military tradition by the Liberal General José María Moncada. However, his professional services were of another nature. First his bilingual talents, and later his politically astute marriage, kept him away from the line of fire. He was posted to the Ministry of Foreign Affairs, where

he worked as a civil servant from 1927 on. This explains where the nickname originated.

2. By 1946, Somoza was owner of forty-six coffee plantations and fifty-one cattle ranches (both breeding and fattening for market), all of them geared to exports.

3. The anti-Somoza demonstrations provoked state intervention in, and eventually the closing down of, the National University, as well as the Conservative newspaper *La Prensa*. Those actions were timely evidence of the National Guard's capacity for repression. Conservative merchants, industrialists, and farmers ceased all of their activities, calling for Somoza's resignation. These were perhaps the forerunners of company work stoppages—also directed by the Conservative bourgeoisie—in 1978, after the assassination of Pedro Joaquín Chamorro.

4. According to some analysts, Luis Somoza—an engineer—was converted into the "political animal" within the family's division of labor. He rose to become deputy and soon thereafter, by the age of thirty, had been elected president of the Chamber of Deputies—while his father held the same position in the executive branch.

5. Anastasio Junior began his studies at the age of eleven at the Military Academy of La Salle in the United States before moving on to West Point. At twenty-one he was granted the rank of major and named inspector general of the army; at twenty-three—by then a colonel—he became director of the Military Academy of Nicaragua; at thirty-two he was appointed commander-in-chief of the National Guard. It should be noted that the career trajectory of Anastasio III was even more rapid, though interrupted definitively by the FSLN.

6. Jaime Wheelock Román, *Imperialismo y Dictadura: crisis de una formación social* (Editorial Siglo Veintiuno, Mexico City, 1978), p. 82.

7. In 1972, cotton amounted to 25 percent of total Nicaraguan exports; meat, 15 percent; and coffee, only 13 percent. See *Informe Banco Central*, 1972.

8. One might recall, as an example, that Somoza III's rise to become director of the Military Academy broke all the rules of army promotion, bypassing the authority, prestige, and seniority of twelve generals. How does one explain that Anastasio III, *El Chigüín* (the little kid), at the age of twenty-seven was a major in the National Guard, with two generals as his assistants? Hundreds of examples of this strange military loyalty could be recounted, and it is within such a framework that the National Guard's enduring loyalty to "the chief" must be examined.

9. Heinz Sonntag, "Hacia una Teoría del Capitalismo Periférico," in *El Estado en el capitalismo contemporaneo* (Editorial Siglo Veintiuno, Mexico City, 1977), p. 67.

6

The Possible Democracy

Introduction

These reflections originated in the new course of political evolution recently under way in the various societies of Central America, for an urgent desire to establish electoral systems has appeared there. That urgency has arisen not so much from an extensive popular demand for substantive democracy as from the need to legalize the leadership role of new authorities in place of ossified political regimes.

An entire set of phenomena—each connected in one way or another with the causes and development of the regional political crisis—has made the problem of democracy the primary subject of both theoretical debate and civic practice. The particular development of the Nicaraguan revolution is at the center of that debate, with highly polarized forces producing contradictory definitions of that process.

There is a paradoxical coincidence in this concern of both warring factions for the trappings of democracy. It is a deceiving coincidence because, on the one hand, among conservative and counterinsurgency strategies, there exists an interest in a simple identification of democracy with elections; whereas, on the other hand, among some ultra-left-wing sectors, a neglect of electoral practice has revealed a lack of comprehension.

Throughout their struggles and in all of their programs, popular forces have always demanded the establishment of democratic forms of government. For their part, the bourgeois groups—who have never practiced democracy—nevertheless continue preaching it in programmatic fashion.

There once existed, in one of many evangelic visions of Marxism, the belief that democracy is bourgeois because the bourgeoisie depends on a democratic constituency. That fallacy must be discarded. At the same time, it must be recognized that the starting point of any analysis on the subject of democracy is to consider it as a historical process. That democratic process evolves in order to establish some form of consensus between those who constitute the majority—occupying a subordinate position in society—and that minority that exercises leadership functions. I will therefore begin these reflections on Central America by recognizing that the democratization processes of any society are historical processes. In other words, social struggles to attain democracy can only be understood within their historical context.

No universal model of political democracy has ever existed. There have only been democratic experiences, which have occurred throughout history. What must be referred to as a predecessor to current political culture is bourgeois democracy, which has also been labeled "liberal" democracy. Both epithets refer to a specific historical period: that marked by the evolution of Western bourgeois society, the confirmation of the capitalist economy, and the predominance of a secular global vision.

In the context of its historical development, liberal democracy was able to appear only in the last phase of the contemporary period. That is, democracy emerged once the modernization of economic life and social relations had become generalized. That societywide evolution was based upon the appearance of a class—the bourgeoisie—capable of establishing an ideological vision of its economic and material interests, thereby endowing private management with a universal dimension.

For the capitalist political order to be legitimate, it must be able to obscure economic exploitation through the free exchange of the market, for that order is based on the exploitation of the dispossessed classes. That legitimacy also depends on the possibility provided by the economic system of transforming the political sphere into one based on free participation and democratic elections. Here it should be remembered that in bourgeois democracies the organization and political participation of the subordinated classes was the result of long and bloody struggles and that the incorporation of the majority was a gradual, cautious process.

Once that incorporation was achieved, however, the political system did not approve the permanent plunder of the exploited classes. Rather, it concealed that exploitation behind the guises of a free labor market and political participation. In addition, ideological and cultural control had the notable advantage of being able to mask existing inequalities. That control thereby veiled conflicts inherent to class relations—relations that by their very nature are opposing and contradictory.

Obviously, liberal democracy has not always functioned so well, even in those democratic societies where capitalism originated. Important works exist on the supposed causal relationship between industrial capitalism and democracy, as well as that between the establishment of bourgeois political systems and the exercise of democratic principles.[1]

But particular conditions were necessary—some of them unrepeatable—in order to attain the levels of popular participation, ideological pluralism, and tolerance of political adversaries exhibited by the major democracies of the postwar period.

There is a theoretical explanation for the emergence of democracy that views that process in relation to exploitation—defined as the extraction of the surplus from some people by others—and that can be expressed in the form of a universal law. That law states that when exploitation takes the form of an exchange of merchandise, assuring freedom and formal equality for all members of the political community, the "class dictatorship" tends to take the form of democracy. That is, democracy serves as the political vestments of a market structure.

The development of capitalism has clearly been associated with the appearance of liberal democracy. To put it somewhat more precisely, the history of Western societies shows that the consolidation of liberal democracy was associated in various ways with the expansion of an urban industrial economy and with the parallel weakening of the landowning nobility.

The bourgeoisie succeeded in making the principles of (economic) freedom and (juridical) equality their own through the market. But, as Pierre Vilar recalled, of all economic freedoms, the first were those of enterprise and exchange. They were strongly advocated by the bourgeoisie at the time as a means of arriving at "the truth of prices."[2] Juridical equality, in its turn, represented a "dissolution" of inherited privilege, thereby making everyone equal in the sphere of competition. Or at least, it enabled and encouraged people to perceive their true condition in that fictitious way. It is in relation to the above that democracy appears as the political consecration of economic equality and freedom—of principles first practiced within the framework of the market, within the fertile kingdom of merchandise.

However, the preceding reflections do not provide the grounds to assert that capitalism is necessarily associated with the triumph of democracy. There are a sufficient number of events from European history to illustrate clearly that the foundations of modern democratic nations were only the product of lengthy struggles, occurring in the midst of societies whose economic development had advanced well into the nineteenth century. The existence of democracy is not only recent, it is also geographically limited.

Finally, within this set of introductory considerations, it would be useful to lay out an additional series of general propositions of lesser theoretical scope. Though they may seem obvious, the presentation of these propositions is worthwhile as a cornerstone to the discussion that follows. From the historical context of contemporary democratic societies it becomes clear that they passed through a stage marked by conditions favorable to political change. Those conditions also favored the gradual establishment of more equal relations and the extension of both a participatory culture and of more tolerant behavior—in other words, the emergence of a democratic authority.

According to some scholars, this had to do with the manner in which the question of the peasant farmer and the problem of agricultural modernization were resolved. They maintain that the resolution of those dilemmas was directly connected to the way in which the social and economic bases of traditional power had been modified. Others stress the character of the social forces that led or opposed political change, focusing on the effective strength of the absolutist tradition as well as the manner in which it could be either broken or modified depending on the relative strength of the new economic interests. Finally, there are those who underline the importance of ethnic, religious, and linguistic homogeneity, identifying the construction of the nation with that of democracy beneath a rubric in which the two results converge and interact.

The problems of liberal democracy—so often used as either a paradigm or a goal—are useful as tools to explore the democratic experiences of Central America. Here references to the great European and/or North American democracies are inevitable, though it is necessary to clarify two points before concluding this introduction.

The first point is that, given a specific level of capitalist development, there are certainly moments in which democratic political relations can be established. Those democratic relations are in each case supported by generalized participation, the search for citizen consensus, and the peaceful resolution of social contradictions. Less "asymmetrical" relations come to the fore, as political subordination and economic exploitation are either confounded or concealed, depending on the hegemonic character of the dominant culture.

The second point is that this historical possibility is inscribed within a wide margin of national variables, of diverse local traditions, and of the nature of particular social struggles. The history of a given movement is ultimately determined by the actions of men and women, limited only by the state of development reached by the forces of production. Multiple variations are possible and, in fact, each experience is unique.

The Conditions for Democracy in Central America

As a consequence of the preceding reflections, those that follow will be informed by the conviction that no historical experience can be used as a model to judge or suggest goals for Central American development. At the same time, however, it is important to consider the conditions under which political democracy can be a historical possibility.

Today, the political structures that distinguish Costa Rica from Guatemala and El Salvador, for example, correspond to processes that have not been easy to identify other than by their results. The objective here, then, will be to analyze how those societies—from relatively homogeneous points of departure—went on to differentiate themselves from one another over the passage of time.

In a generic way, the implantation of capital in the capitalist periphery clearly facilitated the repetition of the historical experiences of those societies with which economic, cultural, and political relations had been established. However, the transfer of economic structures and functions was more successful and profound—via various levels of articulation with the international market—than was the transfer of political institutions and practices. An exception to that rule was the formation of the national state, which emerged parallel to the consolidation of those countries' dependent economic condition.

In any case, the reproduction of previous experiences borrowed from other social orders constitutes a problematic aspect of the region's history. For example, the institutions of the "liberal state" and the ideologies that accompanied them were imitated in the late nineteenth and early twentieth centuries. That duplication was in general unfortunate. The fate of Central American liberalism was such that it did not succeed in developing local ideals of democracy; in fact—and quite to the contrary—it reinforced a number of despotic practices.

The above discussion is only meant to suggest the hypothesis that, with the implantation of capitalism and its primary-export-led development, specific modes and forms marked the establishment of an agrarian bourgeoisie, and of a national state program. The accompanying political structure was based exclusively on a game in which only those who satisfied the prerequisites of citizenship could take part, that is, those who owned land and/or commercial capital. Contradictory advances were made, to a greater or lesser degree, in different Central American countries, and today the results are obviously unequal.

"Real" history, as we know, is not determined merely by underlying economic relations, like an inexorable blueprint. Rather, it is the product of the specific, concrete relations that occur at different moments between groups and social forces over a long period. In order to understand the particularities of that process in its current stage, then, the totality of those social relations must be reconstructed.

In terms of this approach, then, the experiences of Central America—despite its limited physical dimensions—include diverse examples of how "real" history has unraveled through a series of simultaneous and contradictory processes. But those processes—at the general level of universal laws guiding the system—have always had a specific character.

The preceding methodological excursion, then, might serve as a good starting point in order to understand the problems of democracy in Central America. The chapter's main focus will be the persistent questions of why democratic political systems could not be established in four countries of the region and in what ways Costa Rica constitutes an exception.

The best-known explanation of the Costa Rican case revolves around a series of phenomena stemming from the fact that small farms existed in the countryside, producing a supposed rural equality. The present liberal democracy is said to have been built upon that base. The other side of that explanatory coin maintains that the authoritarian tradition and the various dictatorial solutions in the rest of the region have their roots in the early establishment of the large estates (latifundia) and the corresponding social behavior of the landowners.

That explanation maintains that, in a society based on ingrained class privileges, the rigidity of the system converted landownership into a monopolistic source of influence, prestige, and opportunity. Those privileges were sufficient to assure control over those who worked the land. The simplicity of that explanation assigns ontological qualities to the various actors: the small landowners, who possess nascent democratic virtues, and the large landowners, whose structural position in society makes them the bearers of a malevolent, authoritarian upbringing.

The previous reflections have a certain fundamental heuristic value that is not contradicted by their concomitant superficiality. Costa Rican democracy, like that of its authoritarian counterparts in the rest of Central America, was founded through a complex series of factors that were indeed related to the way in which agrarian economies in general are established and develop. That process is particularly relevant in agrarian societies that consolidate themselves as commercial systems oriented almost exclusively toward foreign markets.

Land, as the principal factor of production, also played an important role in that process. That importance was due, above all, to a relative abundance and availability of land in relation especially to investment capital, but also to labor. The diverse combinations of these productive factors were established—not always in accordance with economic rationality—during the course of the implantation of commercial capital in agriculture throughout the region.

In Costa Rica the particular configuration of productive factors determined that control of the *beneficio*—that is, the center for processing coffee before export—would be crucial to the formation of the dominant class. That was so because control of the *beneficio* implied effective control over the channels of intermediation with the mass of small producers, thereby assuring elite regulation of the links between the domestic market and foreign demand. The result was a bourgeoisie formed via control of capital, in the strict sense, more so than land.

This kind of analysis has been made with varying degrees of success[3] and hardly needs further elaboration here. It is enough to remember that, in the rest of Central America, extensive landownership had long been the only available resource that could ensure accumulation; large estates had become "land banks" whose assets represented potential capital. Initially, however, land simply meant wealth and was not hoarded with an eye to financial gain. Control of land meant little more than control of the work force and the reconstitution of social relations, within which personal servitude had been confused with a minimal salary.

In various ways, of course, the establishment of commercial agriculture in Guatemala, in El Salvador, and (partially) in Nicaragua prohibited some forms of extraeconomic compulsion. However, other means of coercion were present in the powers of the state, which arose and strengthened itself by taking up the role of "gendarmerie" in defense of coffee-grower interests.

In Costa Rica, an agrarian bourgeoisie was formed free of conflicts with the Catholic church or indigenous communities, and without the colonial legacies of either land grants for life from the Spanish crown (*enfiteusis*) or common lands (*tierras ejidales*). This in turn facilitated the gradual creation of stable conditions that allowed politics to become a game between contenders who tolerated one another.

But this did not take place because everyone was socially equal, as if the campesino utopia of equality for all had materialized in Costa Rica's Central Plateau. Rather, it was possible because the social classes were able to sustain their conflicts and relations within the confines of a nascent communal identity and because mechanisms were gradually developed for the settlement of their differences.

The various classes, as they formed, were thereby integrated into the emerging nation. Those exercising an as yet inchoate power did not have to resort to the constant use of force and repression in order to maintain control. Other significant factors in the Costa Rican process included the limited demographic and physical size of the society, its common ethnic origins, its relative isolation, and the absence of a colonial bureaucratic tradition.

An interpretation of the history experienced by the rest of Central America is not easy, because the evolutionary process was not homogeneous from one country to the next, despite apparent similarities. The focus will therefore be on the particular conditions that fed the use of force and the overall virulence of each conflict. The essential factor to be analyzed will be the difficulties involved in the creation of a permissive and tolerant culture.

In Guatemala and El Salvador the victory over the past was almost Pyrrhic, given the human suffering that resulted from the reduction of the power of the Catholic church, an essential step toward the consolidation of the liberal state. That suffering was due primarily to the economic dimensions of the conflict.

And in those countries the coffee plantation did not expand by moving into empty spaces, but rather by displacing precapitalist forms of land tenure. That process entailed the disruption of indigenous communities— local societies based on common landownership where campesinos practiced pure forms of subsistence agriculture. Here, the state gradually consolidated itself through the creation and deployment of forces relying on coercion and violence. In the face of social conflict, that state always responded with contempt, castigation, and brutal treatment.

Under these circumstances a paradox appears that has received little analysis. The agrarian-export economy formed and grew slowly in Costa Rica, but extraordinarily rapidly in El Salvador. Guatemala occupied an intermediate position, while Nicaragua was well behind in terms of coffee production. If the bourgeois state of affairs were to be judged by levels of accumulation, the Salvadoran coffee-growing elite (followed by the Guatemalan) would easily have overtaken the Costa Ricans.

However, what makes a producer more bourgeois, in the sense of being more modern—independent of traditional bonds such as the rental of small plots or obligatory worker loans—is not the quantity produced but rather the means used to achieve those levels of production. Equally important is the way in which the value of the product is converted into monetary form and later distributed. In other words, it is not merely a question of what is produced, but of how, and for whom.

At this point it becomes clear that explanations that focus on forms of land tenure are insufficient in order to understand the bases of a functioning democratic society. Other aspects must be considered, such as the degree to which social classes take on modern bourgeois traits and the extent to which the society is capable of integrating those classes, the latter implying some form of ideological management.

Obviously, this has been little more than a sketchy attempt to contribute to an explanation of the socioeconomic dimension of the subject at hand. That dimension clearly lies at the base of the differing results that mark the national histories of each Central American society.

Process and Structure:
Authoritarianism Versus Democracy

Democracy, according to what has been said thus far, is a result of history. If that is indeed true, the following tasks become necessary: first, to determine at what historical moments democracy appears as a possibility; and second, to elaborate what meaning democracy might have for societies like those of Central America. As far as the former is concerned, it is only possible to offer a hypothesis. As for the latter, it is worthwhile proposing a definition. Let us begin with the latter.

In order to avoid confusion about what is meant by democracy in this chapter, we will use a commonsense concept. That concept is based on historical regularities observed in a variety of countries at different times and that are present, to a greater or lesser extent, in what C. B. McPherson has called "liberal democracy" (in order to situate that form of democracy historically).[4]

From that approach, democracy can be recognized as much by the form of its executive branch of government as by its legislative bodies, both of which are directly or indirectly voted into power through periodic elections with universal suffrage. Electors are normally granted the possibility of opting for different political parties. And all of this is carried out within a framework of civil liberties—freedom of speech, of the press, of association, and so on—sufficient to ensure that the right to choose will be effective, that is, relatively free. There also exists a formal, legal equality and some form of protection for minorities, as well as general acceptance of the principle of maximum individual freedom for all.

The previously mentioned hypothesis suggests that democracy as a political regime or as a form of political relations appears as a possibility only when social forces exist that are capable of proposing it as a program, in the sense of an elaborated, collective desire. The nature of democracy as a historical possibility is determined by the concrete combination of at least two key elements: on the one hand, the presence of a political program that is supported by and expresses class interests; and on the other, structural conditions, which are an indication of both the level and the general state of societal development.

A society's democratic possibilities become gradually defined by increasing levels of social differentiation and integration. A minimum degree of political equality combined with wide citizen participation and organization must be practiced regularly and in a genuine fashion. In such a society democracy itself will be held up as an aim of great political or ideological value. It will be appealed to in moments when alliances or opposition movements form—or when conflicts occur—at a political level, whenever the question of political power is posed in either real or symbolic terms.

This hypothesis supposes, more specifically, that the problem of democracy in Central America is a contemporary problem and that the oligarchic period cannot be included in the analysis. That is because the possibilities for democracy did not emerge until after a period in which a transition of state power—from a traditional, exalted oligarchic character into a more modern, bourgeois one—had taken place, and the need for a consolidated authoritarianism had become manifest. For the hypothesis assumes that a political structure is authoritarian only once democratic conditions exist, though that early stage may be nothing more than a preliminary challenge. The long period of oligarchic rule that precedes this stage of nascent democratic yearnings is nothing more than the despotism that accompanies agrarian societies deemed backward in terms of their social development. The preliminary conditions mentioned above are associated with the appearance of social forces capable of pressing for democracy as an interest of the society itself as well as a class interest, as an inherent aspect of their own development.

Some important questions and an initial clarification are pertinent here. In this perspective, could the campesino masses, mobilized by force as actors in an economic process, demand democratic rights such as freedom of organization and free labor? Was the political game necessary in order to mask class exploitation? Which forces had the capacity to choose periodically between various alternatives or to act within a sphere of relatively free political competition?

In Central America, democratic practices such as formal equality, group organization, and the competitive vote began to exist only within social forces or groups enjoying similar levels of economic and cultural privilege. For that reason rivalries and alliances developed almost exclusively within the same class and oligarchical "democracy" was nothing but the initial stage of a process dominated by the authoritarian actors inherent to all forms of class domination.

A second clarification is called for in order to explain the relevance of McPherson's proposal on liberal democracy to a discussion of democracy in Central America. For we do not intend to use the proposal as either a definition or a model. It can be useful, however, as a point of reference, in order to judge when and to what degree those rules of democratic behavior, public or private, have been followed and respected, or whether, perhaps, they have merely been demanded and proclaimed.

Indeed McPherson's hypothesis can serve a double purpose within the framework of this analysis. First of all, elements thereof may be proposed for comparison in order to better describe the functioning of political structures. Second, it can serve to establish, via concrete examples, the various levels of a possible democracy, that is, to historically condition that possibility.

The risk that one runs using this approach is that of referring to those descriptive elements as integral parts of an ideal normative model— implicitly, morally superior—a tendency related to the Eurocentric need of drawing comparisons. The risk, in other words, is that of creating paradigms for Central America composed of Western experiences.

A third clarification refers to the terms *authoritarian* and *despotic*. Authoritarianism can be understood as any exacerbation of power beyond normal limits of control. Those extremes lead to the use of forms and instruments of compulsion; the regime invariably lacks both legal and consensual support. Authoritarianism is thus an intrinsic component of any system of domination. Despotism, in contrast, refers to those earlier stages of Central American history during which popular access to, participation in, or regulation of power—that is, the control and exercise of authority—were neither imaginable nor possible.

When society "grows" vis-à-vis the state and questions it in such a way that the state ceases to be accepted as the primary and sole organizer of that society, forces arise and organize themselves within a new concept of social relations—a concept that presents a potential or real challenge to the existing system of domination and control. That opportunity to challenge the system's capacity for order and coercion—which had appeared to be a "natural" attribute of political or state power—is what gives body to the idea of a possible democracy. However, from the opposite perspective, that opportunity also stimulates the further growth of authoritarian elements within the structure of domination itself.

The previous considerations have been preliminary forms of theorizing about Central American history. But clearly it is insufficient and mistaken to qualify the mid-nineteenth-century political systems and regimes (which arose in the wake of the civil war that broke the Central American Federation) as *authoritarian*, or the period of the "Conservative party peace" in Nicaragua (which followed the defeat of William Walker) as *democratic*.

The authoritarian element is a dynamic, structural component of the preservation and defense of power, but only when the stability and permanence of that power is defied by political forces and when there exists the real possibility of a (democratic) alternative. In this way, democracy is not a stage superior to authoritarianism. Rather, the two together form a political structure that differs from the despotic manner of exercising power.

This mode of reasoning is of the same argumentative nature as that which makes it possible to distinguish between a "primitive" and an underdeveloped society. This reasoning would not permit one, for example, to qualify the socioeconomic conditions of an isolated tribe—exhausting its energies in food gathering, fishing, or itinerant agriculture—as underdeveloped. In that type of society there are no foreseeable options for change; the movement of history has a circular, repetitive nature that serves to guarantee tradition. It is a backward, a primitive society. By contrast, underdevelopment, judged in a historical sense, implies the establishment of various kinds of articulation between societies with different levels of growth. More specifically, that growth means a constant alteration of productive forces. Thus in the latter case constant change is a condition of existence to the extent that capital is expansive by nature.

Central American authoritarian structures and conduct are frequently discussed. Those aspects of the system of domination must be understood, however, in relation to the possibility of another structure and of a different behavior—that is, the democratic possibility. These two theoretical categories, then, will be used to analyze Central American history and to propose an appropriate interpretation of contemporary events in the region.

A final problem is to figure out how and when the preconditions for the establishment of a democratic society began to take root in Central America. That question is as valid as the one that asks about the origins of authoritarianism in the region.

No society is "born" authoritarian, as many Guatemalans imagine, considering the horror of the current counterinsurgency as an extension of Jorge Ubico, Manuel Estrada Cabrera, Gerardo Barrios, and Rafael Carrera; that is, of a long century of dictatorships that succeeded one another almost without pause. Nor is any society democratic—as an extended Costa Rican myth maintains—that feigns amnesia when interpreting various stretches of its own history.

The dichotomy is only valid when presented as a simultaneous contradictory process, and not as two separate, replaceable models. Along those same lines, it is hardly a useful exercise to contrast the two definitions themselves, or to hold up the historical description produced by one perspective in order to judge that produced by the other.

The Democracy Possible Today

The last point goes back to an essential, two-sided proposition: to consider the question of authoritarianism and democracy not only in terms of an institutional power structure, but also as social process, as collective historical action. From that viewpoint, democracy is a form of organizing consensus, much as authoritarianism is a particular form of organizing that consensus by force.

In the history of Central America, the authoritarian perspective as well as the democratic one has its roots in the stage of the liberal revolutions, which were in many ways the region's most important processes of change during the course of the nineteenth century.

There is probably nothing more in line with the tenets of liberal democracy than liberal Central American constitutions, all of which were drawn up during the last fifteen years of the nineteenth century. During that era lines of economic exchange with the exterior, integrated by commercial-export agriculture, were already functioning amid an extended campesino subsistence economy. Between those two economies were areas that produced primarily for the domestic market. The domestic picture of the early primary-export economy was completed by an evolving transportation infrastructure and an elementary system of credit and financing that served to mediate foreign interests.[5] In addition, the presence of foreign capital was already strong at all levels: in agricultural production, in land and sea transport ventures, in the financing of harvests and their sale abroad.

In any case, that economic and social base formed the foundations of the emerging national state, which in turn sought to institutionally encourage and incorporate those characteristics of the changing society that promoted conformity with the concept of nationality. It was a difficult, complex, and contradictory process that produced a system of classes and a power structure most unsuitable to the establishment of peaceful, democratic coexistence. Nonetheless, the importance of the period just described lay with the possibilities that arose for the first time: the possibilities for a democratic organization of both society and the state. That potential only became consolidated—gradually—in Costa Rica, making brief appearances but suffering repeated failures in the rest of the region. Costa Rica's experience was different from that of its northern Central American neighbors as much in terms of democratizing processes—the surfacing of democratic traits—as in terms of the strength of authoritarian behavior and culture. It was at that stage, then, that the region entered the twentieth century.

It should also be recalled at this point that the example presented by the American Revolution and its aftermath—the struggle against colonialism, the construction of political institutions from below, democratic communities integrating popular participation, the U.S. Constitution and free elections—was the model that most inspired the idea of imitating a republican, egalitarian, and liberal society. That influence helps explain the nature of Central American constitutions of the era: the symbolic flowering of an accentuated presidentialism, accompanied by a congress or parliament, an independent judiciary, and elections (initially based on patrimony, then direct, and finally universal). In general, those constitutions took into account both citizens' rights and the duties of the state.

The international moment was also favorable, for in previous years the influence of emerging ideologies and of the French Revolution had taken on a widely endorsed, coherent form in the positivist philosophy of Auguste Comte; the U.S. Civil War had defeated the backward, traditional slave states of the South; and in Mexico the Liberals had defeated French imperialism, followed by the unprecedented successful spread of Benito Juárez's reforms.

Thus the antidictatorial, democratic spirit and faith in popular sovereignty were engrained in every constitution written during the liberal epoch. It is unclear to what extent the coffee-owning bourgeoisie was itself conscious—through its intellectuals and constituent bodies—of the program it wished to undertake. In any case, that bourgeoisie was stimulated by the ties it had established with the expanding international market.

In the final analysis, the bourgeois elite possessed neither the political strength nor the nationalist/statist conviction necessary to create a socially and politically integrated society. The societies that arose were therefore geographically and culturally fragmented—at once separated from and alien to one another—with horizons of political power limited only by the outskirts of the nearest plantation.

In the context of these contradictory circumstances, conditions for the unfolding of democracy were insufficient and unsuccessful, save a few exceptions that ought to be mentioned. This was the period in which that enduring paradox of Central American history appeared: In the very moment that liberal constitutions were passed into law, decidedly authoritarian practices raged beyond control. In effect, state power placed the entirety of its arbitrary and repressive capacity at the service of new opportunities for economic development. Authoritarian features, then, continued to gain strength. They became consistent and organic with the establishment of the political regimes that accompanied the implantation of commercial-export agriculture. Whether Liberal or Conservative, the landowning oligarchy had only a legal conscience of the advantages of democracy; in reality they practiced dictatorship and intolerance with cynical ease.

That historical failure of democracy—an ever-present constitutional objective—originated perhaps in the recurrent, insurmountable conflicts that divided regional factions (agrarian/commercial, Liberal/Conservative) of the bourgeoisie. The dominant class never achieved a sense of unity within its exercise of power.

"Class struggles" were predemocratic at this stage, for they excluded any participation of the dominated. The members of the elite coffee-growing class, conserving backward agrarian values, did not cultivate any conscious respect for the law, which they considered to be little more than a higher form of their own particular designs, a matter of individual will. They had a private vision of the exercise of authority, whose primary function was to prolong their personal management of the plantation. Consequently they tended to lack any real concern for the realm of "public and national affairs." The lack of an effective means of distinguishing between the public and the private was as flagrant as bourgeois blindness vis-à-vis societal contradictions between written law and arbitrary practice.

As a result, the authoritarianism that accompanied the period of liberal revolutions—considered by many the most important stage of the Central American process of economic development—was based upon permanent political and cultural exclusion of the majority. It was a contradictory period of positive law that was not in force, a period marked by an absence of a tolerant political culture, that is, a culture that would permit some changes without necessarily embracing them. In fact, the essential characteristic of the authoritarian regime was that those in command—the dictator, the governing team, the political party— had the effective capacity to avoid political consequences contrary to their own interests in any and all sectors of society.[6]

The Central American practice of authoritarian liberalism was built upon a number of temporarily important factors that together form a collective tradition. First of all, at that time there was a strong desire to leave behind the old Spanish colonial order, for by the end of the nineteenth century a new era seemed at hand.

Second, the leading figures of the day enthusiastically adhered to a rationalist social philosophy that substituted ideas about progress and change for an outmoded social order and traditional values. Finally, the rigid, aristocratic, vision was decisive, justifying the maintenance of old attitudes toward the societal role of the popular masses, and particularly of the campesinos. That elitist conception of politics—fundamental to the liberal way of thinking—supposes, in its everyday expression, that common people are like children: inexperienced and incapable of participating in the game of democracy and freedom.

Why did the postwar era in Central America constitute the end of a historical cycle? In fact, the popular movements that emerged between 1945 and 1948 did not constitute revenge against the past but rather the initial moment of a new cycle that attempted to overcome the most perverse political effects of nineteenth-century liberalism by denying their existence.

It was during that period that the authoritarian features of the system became visible and, moreover, unbearable for important middle-class groups. Their opposition in turn rendered that system vulnerable, as the downfall of several military caudillos—Ubico, Carías and Hernández Martínez—demonstrated. One might describe that preceding period as an extension of the nineteenth century halfway into the twentieth.

The authoritarian tradition of Central American political life has found its contrast in the gradual, persistent establishment and evolution of democracy in Costa Rica. But fleeting sparks of democracy have also marked the experiences of the other countries in the region. It is worthwhile recalling them here, by order of appearance, because they illustrate both the possibilities and the limitations of democracy conceived within an oligarchical context.

The mechanisms of Salvadoran oligarchic democracy were never especially clear; however, they were highly effective in ensuring elitist forms of participation. The internal power game took place among a small group of the major coffee growers. That period began with the government of Francisco Meléndez, from 1885 to 1890, which was followed by those of Carlos Ezeta from 1890 to 1894, Raphael Antonio Gutiérrez from 1894 to 1898, and Tomás Regalada from 1898 to 1903— all of whom came to power via predictable, but tolerated, coups d'état.

From then on, the mechanisms of self-regulation within a single family group permitted a long period of electoral predominance by the Meléndez-Quiñónez family: Carlos Meléndez from February 1913 to August 1914; next his brother-in-law Alfonso Quiñónez, from August 1914 to February 1915; then Carlos Meléndez again from March 1915 to December 1918; followed once more by Alfonso Quiñónez from December 1918 to February 1919; then Carlos's brother Jorge Meléndez, from February 1919 to March 1923; he was succeeded by Alfonso Quiñónez, in his third term, from March 1923 to February 1927; and last, Pío Romero Bosque, the family's lawyer, from March 1927 to February 1931.

Salvadoran democracy was finally put to the test by the election of Arturo Araujo, an aristocrat educated in England and considered an enemy of the traditional oligarchy for his ideas about the working class. Araujo's association with urban trade unions and campesino organizations helped him obtain over 60 percent of the vote in the elections of February 1931. Ten months later, compelled by the dominant groups, General Hernández Martínez headed a military coup that initiated the most authoritarian period in the history of El Salvador. In this case as in various others, the only limitation to democratic theory was its practice.

Democratic possibilities in Guatemala first appeared with the fall of the dictator Manuel Estrada Cabrera and the election of a civilian, Carlos Herrera, who presided from April 1920 to December 1921. But a more extended opportunity came halfway through the century, with the successive free elections of Juan José Arévalo, in 1944, and Jacobo Arbenz, in 1950. This was an important period because of its possibilities for beginning a new stage in the political life of the country. That period, of course, was violently interrupted in July 1954. But Guatemala had yet another opportunity to undertake the democratic path with the government of General Miguel Ydígoras Fuentes. That government was overthrown by another coup d'état in March 1963 when the second electoral victory of Arévalo appeared imminent. In the ensuing period the authoritarian forces—represented by the army as an institution as well as by business groups—prevented all attempts to renew democratic political activity.

The irregularity and unfinished nature of attempts at democracy in Honduras make the possibility of building a deeply rooted democratic tradition seem rather remote. The first important period began with the government of Ramón Villeda Morales, of the Liberal party, from 1957 to 1963. That bipartisan attempt to form a national, civil, and stable power failed, opening the way to a stage of military reformism that lasted until 1972. The results of the latter period were modest and its duration intermediate. In November 1981, in a nonfraudulent election— but within a feeble Honduran voting process—Roberto Suazo Córdova won. The event itself was nothing more than an attempt to return to a traditional elective system; meanwhile, the Honduran military responded by undertaking the task of discrediting those elections as inefficient.

The example of Costa Rica is different. Higher levels of both tolerance for opponents and respect for the law served as the parameters within which a small elite furiously disputed control of executive power. It is clear that fundamental formalities were increasingly respected and that Costa Rican democracy offers a notable example of gradual "perfecting." Indeed that experience was of the sort that can be qualified as a historical construction of a democratic tradition. It would be worthwhile here to recall some examples from the earliest presidential elections. In 1886, President Próspero Fernández handpicked his successor, Bernardo Soto; in 1890 popular mobilization prevented a fraud in favor of Ascensión Esquivel, thereby making possible the victory of José Joaquín Rodríguez, candidate of the opposition. In 1894, only the resort to an electoral college produced the triumph of Rafael Iglesias.

Despite an indirect vote that only became public after 1913, the participation of an important group of intellectuals and liberal politicians managed to reinforce the Costa Rican democratic process. A number of elections, such as the first election of Cleto González Víquez and the last election of Ricardo Jiménez Oreamuno, were by no means free expressions of the will of the entire citizenry. But between 1925 and 1926, Jiménez Oreamuno introduced the secret ballot, voter registration, and an electoral tribunal. Nevertheless, only after 1948 did Costa Rican democracy solidify, in the form of a consensual system, behind elections that had become a vigorous mechanism of legitimation.

In Nicaragua, the possibilities of a democratic course were substantially reduced with the direct military and political intervention of the United States between 1911 and 1933, despite the latter's efforts to carry out and "supervise" free elections. From almost any perspective, Somoza— a direct continuation of the U.S. Marines—from then on constituted the negation of democracy in its most elementary sense.

Only after 1979 were paths opened toward the first real experiences of democracy, in a nation that at the time was hardly enjoying ideal circumstances for the successful implantation of democratic forms of peaceful coexistence. The triumphant popular revolution created conditions for the direct participation of the masses, for moving beyond the mediated forms of representation of the past. That is the contradiction that separates the democratization processes that began after 1979 from those that conservative forces have demanded from abroad.

The Central American political crisis, from this general perspective, is the crisis of an authoritarian system. That system relied on the use of repressive means and failed in the search for both democratic consensus and integration through popular organization. During the postwar period there was a rupture within the context of a continuing antidemocratic tradition, as violence only exacerbated arbitrary, authoritarian practice. Those repressive means were thus put to the test, defied, and—in the case of Nicaragua—overcome. It was that defiance, in the end, that produced rupture.

The political crisis of Central America, then—but particularly of El Salvador, Guatemala, and Nicaragua—has a democratic dimension in a double sense: on the one hand, because it defies the continuation of a persistent, vigorous authoritarianism; on the other, because it proposes a new organization of political life. That latter point is important and will therefore be emphasized in my concluding reflections on the possibilities for democracy in the region.

The problem in building a democracy during this critical stage is that of establishing democratic regimes, that is, a democratic method of government. This would be the first step toward a possible democracy. Central American societies have suffered not only from a limited tradition of law-abiding states but also from an almost total lack of pluralist practice. Public opinion has atrophied without the regular calisthenics of dialogue between rivals. There has been no enduring organizational experience, only that of the great masses, who after years of propriety have finally begun to mobilize themselves from nonpolitical positions.

The difficulty of creating democratic political systems is even greater, because societal heterogeneity has been based on the reproduction of cultural, racial, and even geographic inequalities. Social segmentation has left little room for citizen participation in public life, and therefore formal equality has not had an adequate opportunity to express itself.

The prominence of social hierarchies and their corresponding cultural specificities has been in slow decline, but it is difficult to know how strongly the old forms of consciousness linger on. This uncertainty pertains particularly to Guatemalan and Nicaraguan indigenous groups, but also to subsistence campesino farmers in general—such as those of Honduras—who are isolated or effectively "cornered" in a subpolitical solitude. It also refers to those crushed by poverty, who maintain an untempered distrust for political machinations, those who lost, or never had, confidence in either organized militancy or in the arena of urban politics—long held to be a den of cunning and deceit.

Authoritarian structures in Central America did not destroy democratic institutions, nor did they corrupt the cultural values inherent to that tradition. At times, those institutions simply could not be established. For that reason, the essence of the possible democracy in Central America does not reside in conditions of "the transition to . . . ," but rather "the foundation of. . . ." But that idea is a problematic one. There are no previous experiences that can offer guidelines, nor is there one single type of society capable of giving life and content to democratic ideals. It is a problematic idea because it is posed at the practical level—of action and pursuit—in societies wounded and impoverished by crisis.

The intention in airing these problems is not to abandon a normative vision within the bounds of theoretical analysis, nor to downplay the necessity of strengthening the utopian dimension of praxis. Rather, it is to recognize the need to plant the seeds of an enduring democracy in the firm ground of reality. Here a return to preliminary propositions is worthwhile in order to highlight some of the common operational aspects of authoritarianism in the region:

1. The absence of reliable processes to elect rulers, and in particular of the most elementary form: the appeal to an electoral process
2. The relative difficulty of clearly delineating between the public and the private dimensions of civil society, much less of rendering public conduct coherent and predictable
3. The undefined, and therefore exaggerated, margins for arbitrary action, that is, the impossibility of setting legal standards of discretion for public officials
4. A generalized intolerance, whose nature must also be explained through psychological analysis, whose practice becomes engraved in

the collective memory, and whose implicit "valor" is a by-product of social inequality.

Within such a context, the parameters of political life have moved closer and closer to the laws of war, fed by a kind of ideological and political intolerance closely related to religious fanaticism. The former could indeed be considered a mundane version of the latter, the Central American strain of a "virus" whose spread can in no way be attributed solely to those in command, for it has been contagious and endemic.

A political environment in which some of these failings were not quite so prevalent would clearly be desirable. If the elimination of all of them is desirable, then it is possible, because nothing in the political sphere can ever be achieved unless it is fought for.

Democracy does not advance hand in hand with indicators of industrial growth, nor is it an inevitable product of the modernization of agriculture. Those economic changes only introduce a new set of conditions that make democratic struggle possible. Those struggles for democracy, in turn, carve out a political space whose dimensions are ultimately determined by the distance between the desirable and the possible.

That political space has been created in Central America amid a "diastolic-systolic" cycle of dictatorships that organize fraudulent elections, of civil and military governments that assassinate their opposition, and of political forces that strengthen themselves via the negation of all dialogue. Democracy, then, has been both a historical process and a political space whose durability and perseverance have sustained its possibilities.

The possibility of democracy is in itself the achievement of a possible democracy. The word *possible* is used here in its limited sense of the *attainable*. The political crisis, since 1975 but especially from 1979 on, has accentuated the contradiction between possibility and necessity. That is, what was once posed as an alternative (to traditional authoritarianism) has recently been posed in terms of the ability to take advantage of it. What is necessary here is nothing more or less than the political will to attain the desired changes.

In effect, and contrary to logical analysis, conditions of crisis and war are not the most favorable ones for the successful pressing of democratic demands. Remember that the social forces that suffered the effects of authoritarian policies did not always oppose them with conviction. Though this is another story, the passion for democracy was full of highs and lows, produced perhaps by the modernization hypothesis linked to economic growth.

Expanding a bit on the above propositions, and without going to the opposite extreme, if democracy is not considered to be necessary, the desirable will not be transformed into the possible. The democracy that is possible today in Central America has been produced from the multiform experience of the crisis and resides in the consciousnesses of its actors, culled from their political experiences of subordination, injustice, arbitrariness, exclusion, fear, and death. For within the exceptional context of the Central American crisis, democracy has come to mean the right to defend life.

With the preceding discussion in mind, it is possible to delineate three forms of democracy in Central America today. The first is the Costa Rican, which due to its depth and durability remains exemplary. At the same time it is important to point out that country's "original virtues," which make it a unique and unrepeatable national experience.

A second democratic form is the Nicaraguan, result of a successful revolutionary process. Democracy and revolution are not mutually exclusive, but neither can their compatibility be assumed. The political life of that country has not been built upon the ashes of the Somoza regime, but rather atop its roots. Sandinismo is not democratic merely because it denies the dictatorship's authoritarianism, but because it has achieved where the latter failed: the organization, in a variety of ways, of different social interest groups, their direct participation in a number of civil functions, and other experiences of social mobilization.

The third form is that of Honduras, Guatemala, and El Salvador, which are suitable to be joined in a single category because in all three societies a military withdrawal has taken place, ceding terrain to newly organized political parties. Since 1982, presidential and parliamentary elections have been held and new constitutions have been drawn up. Moreover, diverse conflicts have materialized that, in their development, have intimated the beginnings of a tolerated dissidence vis-à-vis an opposition that has refused to perish.

Such is the meaning of the possible democracy in Central America. Important factors, of course, effectively mitigate that passion for democracy in the region: Unfavorable political forces are many and powerful; economic and social conditions are hardly ideal. Who will be the guarantors of the process? Which forces will be willing to enter into constructive negotiation? Is the present juncture but a fleeting one? There are more questions, but there is also room for optimism.

Notes

1. See Theda Skocpol, *States and Social Revolutions* (Cambridge University Press, New York, 1979); Charles Tilly (ed.), *The Formation of National States in Western Europe* (Princeton University Press, Princeton, N.J., 1975); Reinhard Bendix, *Estado Nacional y Ciudanía* (Amarrotu, Buenos Aires, 1976); Barrington

Moore, *Los Orígenes Sociales de la Dictadura y la Democracia* (Ed. Península, Barcelona, 1973).

2. Pierre Vilar, *Iniciación al vocabulario del análisis histórico* (CRITICA, Grupo Edit. Grijalbo, Barcelona, 1980), pp. 209–210.

3. Numerous explications have been proposed, more or less, in this sense, and an ample bibliography exists. See the recent work of José Luis Vega in *Anuario Centroamericano*, no. 9, and the essay by Héctor Pérez Brignoli, "Crecimiento agroexportador y regímenes políticos en Centroamérica: un ensayo de historia comparada" (mimeograph, San José, 1985).

4. C. B. McPherson, *La democracia liberal y su época* (Alianza Editorial, Madrid, 1981), p. 16.

5. The primary-export period varied from country to country. It lasted from 1850 to 1878 in Costa Rica, 1860 to 1885 in Guatemala, 1865 to 1885 in El Salvador, and 1890 to 1910 in Nicaragua.

6. Adam Preworski, "Democracy as a Contingent Outcome of Conflict" (mimeograph, Chicago, 1984), p. 1.

Index